Travels in Normandy

Vieux Saint Étienne, Caen

Travels in Normandy

Mary Elsy
with
Jill Norman

MEREHURST PRESS
LONDON

Published 1988 by Merehurst Press
5 Great James Street
London WC1N 3DA

Co-Published in Australia and New Zealand by
Child and Associates
5 Skyline Place, French's Forest
Sydney 2086,
Australia

ISBN 1 85391 003 1

Copyright © Mary Elsy 1988

Designed and produced by Snap! Books

Printed in Great Britain by R. Hartnoll Limited

Typeset by Maggie Spooner Typesetting
Illustrations by Anne Forrest
Maps by Sue Lawes
Cover illustration by Malcolm Forrest

Contents

Abbey Church, Fécamp

Introduction
to Normandy

About the Book

The central part of *Travels in Normandy* provides a plan for a 10-day tour of Normandy beginning at Dieppe, circling the region and ending back at Le Tréport, just north of Dieppe.

The itinerary provides a basic route for each day and, for those with time available, offers suggestions for additional trips marked in the text as Detours.

To give added interest to your journey the following section offers background information on aspects of the region — most particularly its cuisine. The final section gives some sample menus and recipes of the region's most typical dishes.

Land Use and Agriculture

Normandy may be divided roughly into two geological areas, separated by a transitional region. It is higher in the east, where some six thousand years ago the invading sea brought in large deposits of chalk and limestone and where later winds spread a fine soil over this base; and lower in the west (the Amorican Massif) which consists chiefly of hard sandstone and granite, formed in the Carboniferous Age, but later considerably eroded, changed and reshaped. Most of the rich open chalklands, orchards and forests of Upper Normandy lie to the north of the Seine and take in the Seine Maritime and Eure departments. Lower Normandy, fertile but less industrial, merges with Brittany and incorporates the Orne, Calvados and Manche departments.

Like its hinterland, the Normandy coast is varied. From Le Tréport to Le Havre are the tall, white chalky cliffs of the Alabaster coast: from Honfleur to Cabourg is the Côte Fleurie, a magnificent stretch of wide sandy beaches, backed by low-lying hills: from Cabourg to Carentan is the Calvados coast, whose flat shores played so important a part in the D-Day landings of World War Two. Lastly comes the Cotentin Peninsula, washed on three sides by the channel and comprised of about 200 miles of glorious sandy beaches and a coastline similar to Cornwall and Britanny. Most Norman beaches are safe for bathing. Many are guarded, but if unguarded, take local advice.

It is this long coastline which determines the climate of the area. High humidity, mild but wet winters ensure the lushness of pastures producing some of the best food in France, certainly pre-eminent in dairy production, its butter, cream and cheese all being world famous. Abundant apple orchards sustain the cider industry, not to mention Calvados, and rich grazing feeds cattle and sheep used for milk, meat and wool. From this local produce the cloth manufacturing industry is most important in Normandy although nowadays the oil industry also plays an important part in the area's affluence. For, despite the terrible devastation of the Second World War, this province has made a remarkable recovery and is even more prosperous than before, due mainly to the hard working and industrious nature of the people. Apart from agriculture and horse-breeding and the industries already mentioned, car manufacture, ship-building, electrical machinery and steel production have all developed with great success.

Mont-St-Michel

History

The name Normandy is derived from those pillaging, plundering pirates, the Northmen, who sailed up the Seine — even as far as Paris — in the 9th century. Later in 911, Rollo, their leader, made a treaty with the Frankish king, Charles the Simple (then 'simple' meant 'honest') at St-Clair-sur-Epte, which gave them the right to occupy a large area of land between the Epte and Avre rivers. It could be described as a gentlemen's agreement (Rollo placed his hands in those of the King of France), as there was never a written treaty. The Epte line later became the scene of many bloody battles.

Those dynamic pagan pirates adopted the Christian religion and the language of the people already living in the region, and became strong exponents of feudalism and champions of the church. Their dukes proved efficient and progressive rulers, making sensible laws and erecting churches, cathedrals and abbeys, and castles all over their province. In 1066, the Duke we know as William the Conquerer was strong enough to cross the channel and take possession of England.

But this Norman success and subsequent wealth threatened the security of France's kings. The union of Normandy and England was broken on the death of William II, and although reunited again, first by Henry I, and later Henry II, it was lost by John to Philippe-Auguste of France in 1204, when he reunited Normandy with France.

In 1346, during the Hundred Years' War (1338-1453), Edward II invaded Normandy and besieged and destroyed Caen. In 1417, Henry V undertook the systematic conquest of the duchy and the resulting occupation lasted until 1450. In 1420, Henry V was recognised as king of France, but his young son's (Henry VI) claim was later disputed by the French Dauphin, Charles VII. After Jeanne d'Arc's intervention at Orléans, the French army forced the English one to raise the siege of the city. Jeanne was subsequently captured (1428), and tried and burnt at Rouen (1431). Nevertheless her victories had given the French fresh hope and paved the way for later recovery. The English army was finally defeated at the battle of Formigny in 1450, and Cherbourg recaptured. In 1469, the last Duke of Normandy was dispossessed by the French king, and the region was subsequently governed as a French province.

Normandy suffered during the Wars of Religion, as many Normans were Huguenots. Caen, an intellectual centre, was strong for Protestantism as were the seaports, which had many links with England and Holland. Although the Edict of Nantes (1598) brought temporary peace to the province, its Revocation (1685) by Louis XIV lead first to persecution, then to massive emigrations of Huguenots from Normandy, mainly to a new life in the New World.

The periods which followed the Hundred Years' War and later the Wars of Religion, were both eras of considerable building in Normandy. In the 15th and 16th centuries, Flamboyant-Gothic had been the popular style (good examples of this can be seen at Rouen, Bayeux and Honfleur), later during the Renaissance a number of town mansions were built and old country mansions ornamented and added to, their fortifications were replaced by parks and formal gardens. But it was the 18th century which proved Normandy's greatest century of building. Many fine châteaux were erected and, as a result of the counter-reformation, Jesuits colleges and churches, episcopal palaces, also town halls but mainly in the formal classical style.

The old pagan northmen of long ago had developed into a hard-headed, business-like, efficient and rather conservative people, who favoured reforms, but disliked excesses. During the French Revolution, Caen was the centre of the Girondins, the party of moderation who resented Parisian domination. Some Normans, opposed to the new French republic, joined the armies of the Vendée and the Chouans, who hid in the wooded parts of the Cotentin, where they fought a sort of guerilla war against the revolutionary forces.

During the 19th century, a period of peaceful expansion and prosperity, railways were built and Rouen was linked with Paris (1843), as was the sea coast. The Duchess of Berry started a vogue for sea bathing at Dieppe, a fashion which spread, especially along the nearby Côte Fleurie. Wide skies, good light and long attractive seascapes drew many artists, especially the Impressionists, to the Normandy coast to paint.

Upper Normandy and Le Mans were occupied by the Germans during the Franco-Prussian war (1870-71): allied troups were stationed in Normandy during World War One. Normandy's greatest ever disaster, however, came in World War Two, first in 1940, when the Germans invaded France, and then in 1944, when the beaches along the Côte Nacre on the Calvados coast and nearby eastern side of the Cotentin peninsula became the bridgehead of the allied invasion of Europe.

Famous Names

It may seem strange that such a practical and efficient people as the Normans should have produced so many good writers, men of letters and artists. But one must remember that both learning and art originated in and were nurtured by monasteries — and Normandy had a number of monasteries. A university was founded at Caen and a Jesuit college at Rouen in the 15th century.

Pierre Corneille (1606–1684), the great French classical writer, born into a legal family at Rouen, qualified for the bar and became a magistrate there. He was a pioneer of psychological tragedy. His taste for grandeur and truth were always tempered by Norman restraint. *Bernard de Fontanelle* (1657–1757), a nephew of Corneille also from Rouen, achieved success as a scientific populariser. His religious scepticism led to the philosophic movement of the *Encyclopaedists*, who were to dominate French thought after 1750. *Gustave Flaubert* (1821–1880), another Rouennais, was a Romantic and lover of words, but his disgust with contemporary life made him depict in minute detail the drab stupidity of his Norman town in 'Madame Bovary'. He spent most of his life working hermit-like at his father's house at Croisset. Flaubert was instrumental in establishing the realistic novel which was to dominate French literature for the next 30 years. *Guy de Maupassant* (1850–1893), the acknowledged master of the realistic short story, was much influenced by Flaubert. He is at his best when writing of the middle classes and the peasantry of his native Normandy. Man, in his cynical view, is cut off from both the beast and angel and is incapable of developing in either direction.

Nicholas Poussin (1593/4–1665), the originator of the French classical style in painting, came from Normandy, and from a family which had once been noble but which had been reduced to peasantry by the civil war. He pursued his artistic career apparently against his parents' wishes, spending some time in Paris, working under various masters and studying the royal collection. He went to Rome about 1624, where he purified his style, came under the influence of the Venetians, and established his reputation. He was lured back to Paris in 1640, lodged at the Louvre and given much work. However, he disliked the intrigues, the cold climate and his eminent patrons and returned to Rome. Poussin wished his work to be a rational expression of ideas.

The English painter, *Richard Parkes Bonington* (1801/2–1828, precociously gifted, emigrated to France in 1817. His freshness of colour — he managed to capture the wetness of Normandy beaches — and handling of subjects in his small landscapes and costume pieces influenced artists as notable as *Delacroix* and certainly *J.F. Millet* (1814–1875), born at Gruchy, in his paintings of country life around La Hague. Millet was of farming stock and brought up to work in the fields. After studying art at Cherbourg, he was eventually to make the realistic depiction of the countryside and peasant folk his life's work. In 1848, the village of Barbizon, near Fontainebleau, became his home, and the school of artists who gathered round him became the Barbizon school.

Claude Monet (1840–1926), son of a grocer at Le Havre, made his first contact with the professional art world when he met Eugène Boudin (1824–1898) 'King of the Skies', whose beach scenes anticipated Impressionist clarity of colour, although he did not use Impressionist techniques. Monet's god was light. He believed that colour could only be perceived in terms of light and its movements. Pointillism (divided tints with little touches of colour) was a later development of Impressionism. *Georges Seurat* (1859–1891) and *Paul Signac* (1863–1935) pioneers of this method came to Normandy to study its landscapes.

The Epicure's Guide

Normandy is a land of plenty, one of the great gastronomic provinces of France. It is a prosperous agricultural region, producing rich milk, cream, butter and cheese, meat and poultry, fruits, cereals and vegetables, and from the fishing ports of the long coastline come great catches of fish and shellfish. It is also the land of cider and Calvados, a robust, yet fragrant brandy distilled from apples.

These are the foundations of Norman cooking, to be found in every farm, inn or restaurant across the province. Yet within the region traditional differences are preserved; individual towns and villages are renowned for certain produce and dishes.

To the west, adjoining Brittany, lies Lower Normandy. Here the landscape is rugged and wooded, farms are set in deep valleys. Fine-flavoured sheep are reared on the salt meadows of the rather bleak Cotentin peninsula that juts out far into the English Channel. In the centre of the province is the Auge valley, often called 'the garden of Normandy'; an undulating landscape of extensive apple orchards and rich green pastures grazed by brown and white cows.

The Seine meanders across Upper Normandy to reach the sea at Le Havre. To the north and east of the river, bounded on the other side by the Channel coast, is the Pays de Caux, a flat plain well suited to arable farming on a large scale. Belts of wheat, flax and sugar beet are interrupted by occasional areas of woodland and villages of substantial stone houses.

Rouen, the lovely city on the Seine, is the capital of Upper Normandy: Caen, its fine abbeys overlooking the Orne, the capital of Lower Normandy. These cities are gastronomic as well as regional capitals; both have given their names to dishes that are prepared throughout France — canard à la rouennaise and tripes à la mode de Caen.

The Rouennaise duck is a cross between wild and domestic breeds, raised in

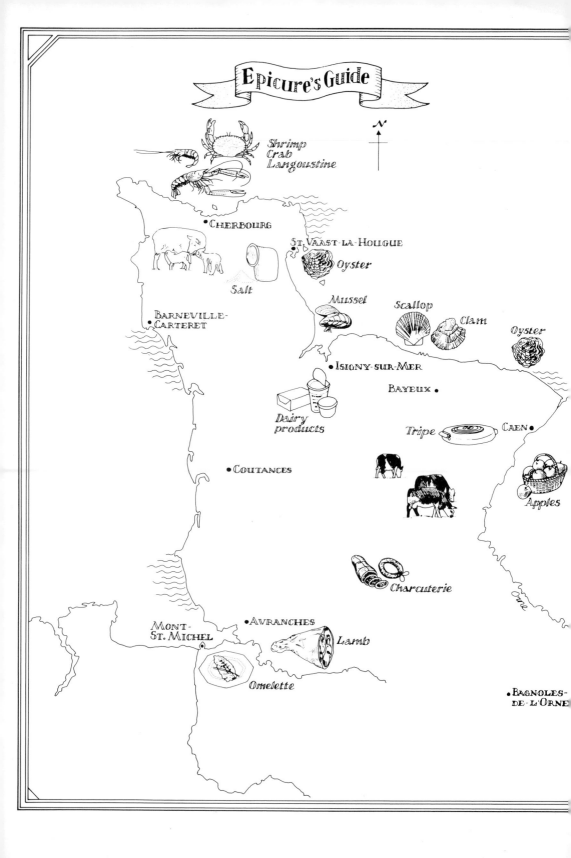

Epicure's Guide

N

Shrimp
Crab
Langoustine

CHERBOURG

ST. VAAST-LA-HOUGUE

Oyster

Salt

Mussel

Scallop

Clam

Oyster

BARNEVILLE-
CARTERET

ISIGNY-SUR-MER

BAYEUX

CAEN

Dairy
products

Tripe

COUTANCES

Apples

Charcuterie

Orne

MONT-
ST. MICHEL

AVRANCHES

Lamb

Omelette

BAGNOLES-
DE-L'ORNE

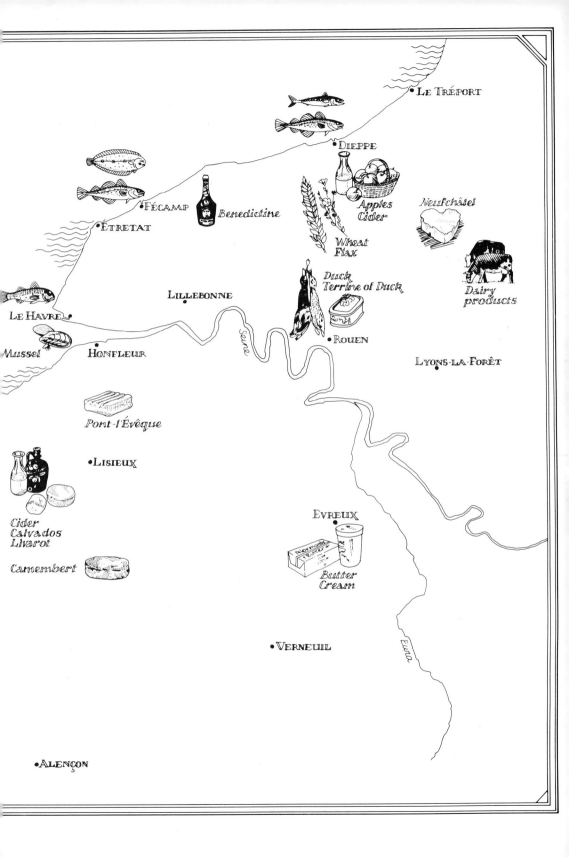

LE TRÉPORT

DIEPPE

Apples
Cider

Neufchâtel

FÉCAMP   Benedictine

ÉTRETAT

Wheat
Flax

Dairy
products

LILLEBONNE

Duck
Terrine of Duck

Mussel

LE HAVRE

ROUEN

LYONS-LA-FORÊT

HONFLEUR

Seine

Pont-l'Évêque

•LISIEUX

EVREUX

Cider
Calvados
Livarot

Butter
Cream

Camembert

•VERNEUIL

Eure

•ALENÇON

large flocks around the towns of Yvetot and Duclair. Canard à la rouennaise belongs to restaurant cookery. The traditional recipe requires the duck to be strangled to conserve the blood in the body, so that the flesh remains quite red, even after cooking, and the flavour is rather gamey. The sauce is made with cider, stock and the blood and liver of the duck. Canard au sang, or pressed duck, is a variant of the Rouen recipe that was adopted by top Parisian restaurants in the late nineteenth century.

Most of the grand restaurants of the province serve the rare, roast duck with its deep rich sauce. You may also be offered spit-roasted duck, duck braised in cider, or the excellent terrine of duck that is another speciality of Rouen.

Tripes à la mode de Caen is also a dish to eat on a visit to Normandy, rather than one to cook at home. Tripe has always been eaten in restaurants or bought as a take-away dish from the butcher or charcutier to be reheated at home. The prepared tripe — ox stomach in Normandy — is cooked for 10 to 12 hours with calf's feet, onions, leeks, carrots, herbs, cider and Calvados in a special tripière, a flat round earthenware dish with only a small opening in the top to prevent evaporation in the long slow cooking process. Each year in Caen a competition is held to find the best tripe recipe in the province and the winner is awarded the Tripière d'Or.

Normans still eat steaming bowls of tripes à la mode de Caen mid-morning, especially on market days. Other tripe specialities to look out for are tripes en brochette — little packages of tripe and calf's foot on skewers — from La Ferté-Macé, and tripe and ham parcels from Coutances.

Charcuterie is the mainstay of Norman hors d'oeuvres and most parts have their own recipe for a sausage, pâté or brawn. The pigs are fed on windfalls of apples and pears, which gives the flesh a fine, sweet flavour. The best Norman charcuterie are boudins — black and white puddings, the black made with pig's blood, the white with milk and breadcrumbs mixed into the meat. Both boudin noir and boudin blanc are traditional dishes eaten on Christmas Eve with potato purée and sautéd apples — a dish called Boudin avec Deux Pommes.

The picturesque town of Mortagne-au-Perche, situated on a hill overlooking the valleys that are the home of the Percheron horse, is the centre of the black pudding world. Pudding makers from all parts of Europe gather here each year for 3 days during Lent to sample and judge each other's wares.

From Vire come the famous large and small tripe sausages — andouilles and andouillettes respectively. These lightly smoked, black skinned chitterlings can be bought from all the charcutiers, and many restaurants in the little town serve them grilled with potato, apple or sorrel purée, to be washed down with cider.

In Cherbourg, at the tip of the Cotentin peninsula, or in Avranches or Mont-Saint-Michel make sure to try the excellent roast or grilled lamb, often described on menus as gigot des grèves du Mont-Saint-Michel or gigot de pré-salé. The sheep graze on the coastal pastures and the salt deposited by the tides gives the meat a succulent and delicate flavour of the sea.

Mont-Saint-Michel is also noted for its omelettes. The successor to la Mère Poulard's famous restaurant (she died in 1913) still serves omelettes according to her 'recipe'. More unusual and interesting is the boudin served in some restaurants in Avranches. The sausage is made from pike and sweetbreads, lightly poached and then baked in a creamy fish sauce.

Today we think of butter and cream as the foundation of Norman cooking, but in fact their use is fairly recent. At the beginning of the century the most common cooking medium was graisse normande — a preparation made by simmering together beef kidney fat, root vegetables and herbs until the fat clarifies and is permeated with the flavour of the vegetables. It is seldom used now, perhaps because it takes time, though not much trouble to prepare. In any event, with such superlative butter and cream to hand, who can blame the Norman cook for using them as the basis of the cooking of the province. Even in our cholesterol-conscious age you will still find dairy products used to create traditional and new dishes.

The taste of Normandy butter is unmistakable. It is closer to the sweet, natural flavour of thick cream than any other kind. It imparts a particularly fine flavour to any dish and is superb for making sauces and for baking, as well as for spreading on bread. Crème fraîche, the slightly sourish thick cream, now made commercially, but until recently made in every household, is used extensively to make sauces, to accompany vegetables, or a bowl may be put on the table to serve with fresh fruit or a dessert of pancakes or pastry filled with apples.

Butter and cream are made throughout the province; Gournay and Neufchâtel are the main centres in the Pays de Bray, Évreux in the Vallée de l'Eure and Isigny in the Pays d'Auge. The last region is perhaps the most renowned for its dairy produce; at Isigny they claim that the salty sea air is partly responsible for the special flavour of their butter. Certainly the local butter and cream are used to advantage in dishes such as poulet vallée d'Auge, côte de veau vallée d'Auge or darne de saumon à la mode d'Isigny. Any product labelled specialité de la Vallée d'Auge is considered to be of the very best quality.

The third great Norman dairy product is of course cheese. The native breed of cows with hides of brown, ivory and white, and brown 'spectacles' around the eyes, were brought by the Viking invaders a thousand years ago. Through careful breeding they produced prodigious quantities of milk — a good cow gives 30 litres (6½ gallons) of milk a day. And Normandy has six million cows. The fat content and volume of milk from every cow is measured against its food ration — the acreage of grazing and type of grass; in Normandy grass (there are four million acres) becomes a commodity when it is converted by cows into milk, cream, butter and cheese.

For centuries the excess milk from Norman cows has been transformed into naturally fermented soft cheeses, most of them with a creamy centre and a white-coated crust. Today Normandy produces about half of the soft fermented cheeses made in France.

The best known is Camembert which takes its name from a tiny village just to the south of Vimoutiers. The cheese can be traced back to the twelfth century and was perfected by a farm woman, Marie Harel, around 1791. But Camembert was only known in the region until in 1890 a Monsieur Ridel invented the little chipboard boxes that enabled the cheese to be shipped over long distances. Before this, Camembert was sold wrapped in straw and spoiled if sent even as far as Paris.

The best Camembert is made with unpasteurized milk with a minimum fat content of 45% and it is cured for at least a month. The small disc-shaped cheese should have a downy white surface and feel supple. When it is mature the crust may have touches of russet-red. It can be eaten young when the centre looks chalky white or kept until the flavour is more developed and the centre softer and more creamy in colour. A good unpasteurized Camembert has a slight tangy smell; a smell of innocuous mould indicates a factory cheese made with pasteurized milk. The cheese should have no trace of ammonia or mildew.

The label VCN (Véritable Camembert de Normandie) signifies a high quality cheese from the departments of Calvados, Eure, Orne, Manche or Seine-Maritime. Authentic Camembert are made only in this region, although many other parts of France, and indeed many other countries now produce pasteurized Camembert.

The 'road of great cheeses' runs through the Auge valley from Camembert and Vimoutiers northwards through the other cheese towns of Livarot and Pont-l'Évêque to the English Channel. Livarot and Pont-l'Évêque are both ancient cheeses, made in the style of the early cheese called angelot, said to have been the favourite of William the Conqueror. They are longer lasting cheeses than Camembert because of the way they are made and matured.

Livarot is a cylindrical cheese with a smooth, glossy deep red-brown rind, which results from frequent washings with salty water. The colour comes from brushing with an annatto solution. Livarot cheeses are matured for three months in humid cellars from which fresh air is excluded. The cheese has a strong smell and a spicy flavour. It is usually banded with strips of sedge (marsh grass) and boxed. Petit Lisieux, also known as Demi-Livarot, is a smaller cheese, made in the form of a flattened cylinder. It has a similar spicy tang, and Livarot and Petit Lisieux need a robust wine or the local cider or calvados to accompany them.

Pont-l'Évêque is a square cheese with a smooth golden rind, acquired by frequent washing or brushing. It has 50% fat content and like Livarot and Petit Lisieux is cured in humid cellars, but only for six weeks. It has a pronounced flavour and smell. Other closely related cheeses to look out for are Pavé d'Ange (also called Pavé de Moyaux) and Carré de Bonneville. One other cheese from the Auge valley should be mentioned — Mignot, a disc-shaped farm cheese with a 40–45% fat content, a red rind and a white interior. Its distinctly fruity taste goes admirably with cider.

The other important cheese-producing region is the Pays de Bray. As well as supplying Paris with most of its fresh milk and cheese, Bray is France's major producer of fresh white cheese, most of it coming from the Gervais factory at Gournay. Virtually all the cheeses of this area are soft, fresh cheeses, made in small dairies or factories.

Excelsior, a cheese with a mild creamy flavour, invented at the end of the nineteenth century, is the begetter of many modern double and triple cream cheeses such as Brillat-Savarin, Fin de Siècle, Magnum, Parfait and Suprême, all made in this region. Monsieur, also invented at the end of the last century by a farmer appropriately called Fromage, is an excellent cheese — a soft cylindrical cheese with a white rind spotted with red, a penetrating odour and a delicious nutty flavour, not unlike Brie. La Bouille is a very similar cheese with a richer taste due to its longer maturing period.

Gournay and Carré de Bray are small cheeses, one a disc, the other square, with a mild, slightly salty taste. Gournay is sold on traditional straw mats. The oldest cheese from Bray is Neufchâtel which can be traced back to medieval times. It comes in different shapes — square, heart-shaped, cylindrical — and has a white, bloomy rind and a somewhat salty flavour.

All these cheeses are at their best in summer and autumn when the pastures are richest.

Moving on to the coast, there is a change in emphasis. Fishing, not farming, is the principal activity. The ports of Dieppe, Fécamp, Le Havre, Honfleur and Cherbourg all have fishing fleets and there are the early morning markets where you can watch fishermen and auctioneers shouting their prices to restaurateurs, fishmongers and merchants from as far inland as Paris. Later in the morning the housewife, or browsing tourist, will find a spectacular array at the local fish stall or shop. Flat fish such as brill, turbot and sole; cod, hake and dogfish, gleaming mackerel, red and grey mullet, even John Dory are displayed on ice and seaweed with a profusion of langoustines, small lobsters (called demoiselles de Cherbourg by the locals), prawns of all sizes, small grey shrimps and crabs. To complete the display there are oysters from St-Vaast and Courseulles, mussels from Isigny and Villerville, scallops, tiny cockles and several types of clams from beds along the coast.

Every coastal town and village has restaurants that specialize in seafood and fish dishes, and inland as far as the Ile de France some Norman fish is likely to appear on the menu of any good restaurant. Choose a busy little restaurant by the sea and start your meal with a seafood platter, perhaps followed by that Norman speciality, sole. In Dieppe it is cooked à la dieppoise in a wine and cream sauce, garnished with prawns or crayfish, mussels and mushrooms. Further along the coast sole à la deauvillaise has a cider, cream and onion sauce. You may also find the simple matelote of sole, with cider and mussels, probably the starting point for the grand restaurant dish, sole à la normande, for which every chef seems to have his own recipe, attempting to outdo all others in offering an array of luxurious garnishes. Since the dish was invented in the nineteenth century oysters, mussels, scallops, crayfish, shrimps and truffles are all found in varying combinations in the rich cream sauce.

Other fish dishes to sample include cold mackerel from Dieppe; Fécamp cod, coated with breadcrumbs, fried and served with sautéd apples and Bénédictine (Fécamp abbey is where the liqueur was created in the sixteenth century); lobster simmered in cream; eel stew and mussels in cream sauce.

In addition to grasslands and cows, orchards are a common feature of the Norman landscape, particularly in Lower Normandy. Apples and pears are grown in dozens of varieties. Reinettes, yellow streaked, russet apples with a sweet, crisp taste are the best eating apples. Calvilles are popular for pastries and desserts. Most of the other varieties are pressed to make cider.

Normandy has no wine; the province is too northerly for grapes to ripen successfully. A few hundred years ago wine was made here, but it was probably rather thin and acidic. Instead of trying to grow vines, Norman farmers have wisely turned to cider making. Apple trees flourish in the Norman landscape and climate, and cider is made to a very high standard.

Although cider is made throughout the province, the best comes from the Pays d'Auge. Norman cider may be golden or reddish, sweet or dry, sharp or full bodied. Cidre bouché, corked cider, is dry and slightly sparkling. It is bottled with a champagne cork and wire fastener because the fermentation is allowed to finish in the bottle. Good cider can be bought everywhere in Normandy and will be drunk with most meals by the Normans.

Calvados is apple brandy distilled from cider. It is subject to appellation controllée laws concerning its manufacture and labelling. It may be produced by a single distillation in a continuous still (as grain whisky is produced in Scotland) or double distillation in a pot still. Eleven areas are permitted to produce Calvados, and in ten of them it is made in a continuous still and is labelled Calvados, appellation reglementée. In the eleventh, Pays d'Auge, the best cider, cidre de la Vallée d'Auge, is double distilled and the Calvados is labelled appellation Pays d'Auge controllée.

To make Calvados, the apples are washed and pressed to a pulp from which the juice is extracted. The juice ferments for about a month, and as cider it is then transferred to the still. The clear distillate is moved to oak barrels where it is left to age. During the aging process the Calvados takes on its deep golden colour from the oak cask. Some distillers age their Calvados for only twelve months before bottling, others may leave it in the cask for ten years or more. Great Calvados acquires its bouquet from the oak barrel and improves enormously for being left longer in the wood.

There are three occasions when a Norman drinks Calvados: early in the morning with a black coffee (café calva is what you ask for), midway through a substantial meal, when the eating stops for the trou normand or Norman hole (a glass of Calvados is taken to aid digestion and make room for more courses) and, of course, as the perfect end to a good Norman meal.

Handy Tips

HOW TO GET THERE FROM THE UK
The Itinerary begins at Dieppe.
By Air Main airports at Paris or Rennes (Brit. Air), can be used to connect with either local air or rail services. It is advisable to reserve a hire car at your destination in high season.

By Rail Boat trains leave Victoria, London, regularly for Dover–Calais, Folkestone–Boulogne and Newhaven–Dieppe. From Waterloo, London, to Weymouth–Cherbourg is another possibility. For extra speed Calais and Boulogne are both served by Hovercraft.

By Car The most common way to Normandy is on a Car Ferry. Advisable to pre-book in summer. Relevant channel ports are Dieppe, Calais, Boulogne, Dunkerque, Le Havre, Cherbourg and St. Malo.

WHEN TO GO
Any time from Easter to the end of September. In a good Autumn, warm sunny weather will last to the end of October.

Try to avoid travelling on or just before or after a bank holiday (see below). The worst time for traffic is the first weekend in August, when nearly every French family is on the move.

HOTELS
It is advisable to book hotels in advance especially between July and September.

CAMPING AND CARAVANNING
There are some wonderful sites throughout Normandy. Buy the green Michelin Camping and Caravanning guide for addresses. Unlike dreary England even the smallest of sites has electricity. N.B. Don't forget your Caravan Club of Great Britain registration carnet.

DRIVING

Driving on the right is usually no problem, the danger only comes when returning to the road from a car park, a petrol station and of course at roundabouts. Until recently priority was always given to those approaching from the right. This custom is fast changing and roundabouts can therefore be treated in the English style, but beware drivers turning from small roads in towns and country lanes. Traffic police can be tough even on foreign motorists who are caught speeding, overshooting a red light or failing to wear seat-belts, so take care. Seat-belts are obligatory everywhere in France outside town limits.

ROAD NUMBERS

The French government, which used to be responsible for numbering all the roads in France, has started to hand over the responsibility to the individual départements. In their wisdom the individual départements have in some cases decided to renumber the roads and as you can imagine this process is not only slow but confusing. I have tried to be as correct as possible with the road numbers, but you may unfortunately find some discrepancies. For example you could come across a road marked as the N137 when it is really the D937.

SPEED LIMITS

Autoroutes	130 kmph (80 mph)
Other Roads	90 kmph (56 mph)
Dual Carriageways	110 kmph (68 mph)
Built-up areas or as directed by signs	60 kmph (37 mph)

Autoroutes nearly all have periodic tolls (péages) and can be expensive on long journeys.

THE METRIC SYSTEM

Kilometres — for road distances 8 km equals 5 miles thus:

Km:miles	Km:miles	Km:miles	Km:miles
3:2	8:5	40:25	90:56
4:2½	9:5½	50:31	100:62
5:3	10:6	60:37	125:78
6:3½	20:12	70:44	150:94
7:4	30:18	80:50	200:125

BANK HOLIDAYS

New Year's Day	1st January
Easter Monday	Variable
Labour Day	1st May
V.E. Day	8th May
Ascension Day	6th Thursday after Easter
Whit Monday	2nd Monday after Ascension
Bastille Day	14th July
Assumption	15th August
All Saints (Toussaint)	1st November
Armistice Day	11th November
Christmas Day	25th December

BANKS

Banks are shut on Saturdays and Sundays, except in towns with a Saturday market, when they open on Saturday and shut on Monday. Banks also close at midday on the eve of bank holidays. Banking hours are normally 8 a.m.–12 noon and 2–4.30 p.m. When changing cheques or travellers' cheques remember your passport and Eurocheque encashment card or other internationally recognised cheque card.

SHOP OPENING TIMES

These vary according to a) season b) type of shop c) size of town. In most places shops are open on Saturday, but may be shut on Monday. Food shops (baker, butcher, general store) tend to shut later than others, sometimes as late as 7 p.m., some open on Sundays and bank holiday mornings.

RAILWAYS

S.N.C.F. — Société Nationale de Chemin de Fer. The trains are generally very clean, comfortable and punctual. It is best to buy tickets in advance from mainline stations or travel agents. Seats can be reserved on main lines. Hire cars can be booked in advance in most large towns. Bicycles can be hired at stations. Men over 65 and women over 60, on production of their passport, can obtain a 'carte vermeil' entitling them to a 50% reduction on non-rush hour trains.

Note: Many stations have automatic punch ticket machines (red machine) on the platform, this dates your ticket. If you do not get your ticket punched by one of these machines you can be charged again, plus a fine of 20%, so be careful.

MONUMENTS AND MUSEUMS

Opening times and prices of admission have not been included in this book, as they are subject to change. All places mentioned are open to the public and will charge a few francs admission. Normally they will be open from Easter to the end of October, from 9.30–12.00 a.m. and from 3–5 p.m.

Note: Guided tours will cease admission half an hour before closing. Check with the local tourist office for details.

KEY TO ITINERARY

Ratings are for prices/room/night.

★★	Reasonable	★★★★	Expensive
★★★	Average	★★★★★	Very expensive

Names of the hotels and restaurants which are the first choice of the author are distinguished by the following symbols:

Lunch   Dinner

TEXT MAPS.

The map on p. 32-3 shows the complete 10-day itinerary.
Detailed journey maps are as follows:
Days 1 & 2: pp. 42-3.
Days 3, 4 & 5: pp. 54-5.
Days 6 & 7: pp. 86-7.
Days 8 & 9: pp. 104-5.
Day 10: pp. 124.

The Itinerary

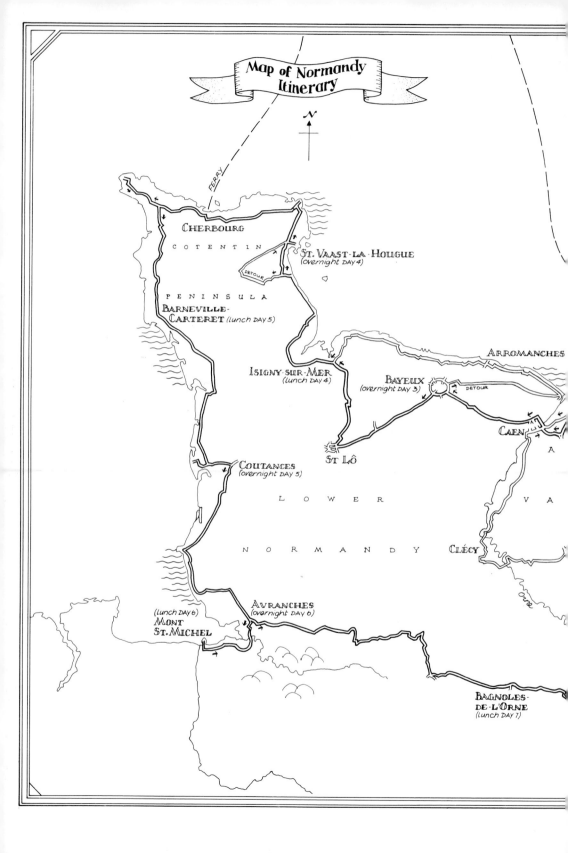

Map of Normandy Itinerary

N

FERRY

CHERBOURG

COTENTIN

ST. VAAST-LA-HOUGUE
(overnight DAY 4)

DETOUR

PENINSULA

BARNEVILLE-
CARTERET (lunch DAY 5)

ARROMANCHES

ISIGNY-SUR-MER
(lunch DAY 4)

BAYEUX
(overnight DAY 3)

DETOUR

CAEN

A

ST LÔ

COUTANCES
(overnight DAY 5)

L   O   W   E   R

V   A

N   O   R   M   A   N   D   Y   CLÉCY

Orne

AVRANCHES
(overnight DAY 6)

(lunch DAY 6)
MONT
ST. MICHEL

BAGNOLES-
DE-L'ORNE
(lunch DAY 7)

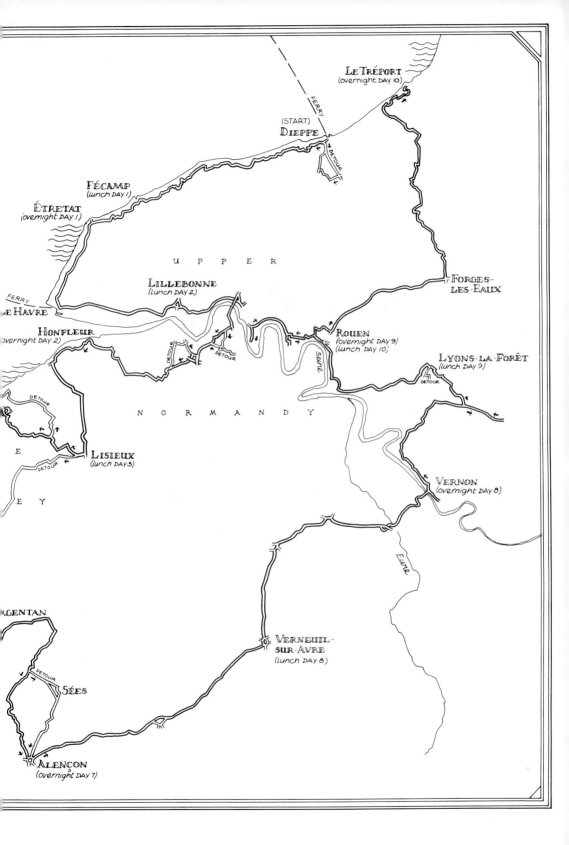

Cliffs of Étretat

The Itinerary

DAY 1

Dieppe to Étretat: approx 50 miles.

If you arrive early in the morning then explore the bustling port of Dieppe to get your first flavour of France. Alternatively you may wish to take a short trip south of Dieppe to the cider-apple valleys of the Scie and Varenne. From Dieppe follow the coastal route southwards as it winds through the hamlets and picturesque scenery of the Alabaster Coast to Fécamp. After lunch it is pleasant to meander through the steep, narrow streets of this old cod-fishing port before a short drive further down the coast to the Edwardian resort of Étretat.

Arrive at Dieppe

Dieppe

Dieppe set in the bend of Arques river is one of the safest and deepest of the channel ports. In fact, its name comes from 'Deope', Saxon word for 'deep'. It is also my favourite arrival port in France. After passing beaches and gardens, the ship seems to plunge straight into the heart of the town. Although cafés and seafood restaurants are probably Dieppe's chief attraction for English visitors — some of the best value ones are to be found along Quai Henri IV, near the port — the town itself is worth exploring. If you arrive on a Saturday, do not miss a visit to the huge colourful market in the Place Nationale, one of the best markets in Northern France and which offers a wide range of the region's produce.

Not far from Paris, Dieppe is one of France's oldest seaside resorts. Its many picturesque corners once attracted the attention of artists such as Turner, Beardsley, Pissarro and Sickert. So, follow in their footsteps and view what inspired them — the ports (passenger, fishing and commercial); old Dieppe around Puits-Salé Place, and its church, St Jacques (13th- to 16th-century). Note the freize around the sacristy door, which shows a file of Brazilian Indians, a reminder of Dieppe's explorers. It comes from Jean Ango's palace, which was destroyed by the British naval bombardment of Dieppe in 1694 (during the war for the League of Augsburg). Jean Ango, the Parmentier brothers and Verrazano (Florentine) are four well-known master mariners and explorers from Dieppe.

Some of Dieppe's attractiveness is due to the British, although unintentionally. After the above-mentioned bombardment, the town was rebuilt in the 18th-century style, a fortunate period for architecture. Two centuries later, most of the nondescript hotels and boarding houses, which had mushroomed up along the front beside the dunes, shingle beach and sea, were destroyed by the ill-fated Dieppe raid of the last war — Operation Jubilee in 1942.

This front has been newly laid-out, and now includes a complex of tennis courts, miniature golf, children's playground, heated open-air sea water swimming pool, and casino (the latter also comprises a night-club, cinema and dancing in high season). The former casino, incidentally, was dynamited by the Germans after the Dieppe raid to improve the efficiency of their coastal defences. The 15th-century castle, overlooking the front, has a museum of sculpture, local archeological finds, ship's models, maps, naval instruments, pottery and ivory (a legacy of Dieppe's long trade with Africa and the Orient).

Dieppe makes a good centre for small excursions along the coast and into the hinterland and is within easy reach by car of the forests of Eu, Arques and Eawy. You can drive to Paris from Dieppe, N27 to Rouen and along the Seine valley, or you can drive there via the Eawy forest — one of the most beautiful stretches of beeches in Normandy. Or, longer, via Forges-les-Eaux (see p. 127) through the forests of Bray and Lyons.

Detour

Dieppe lies just north of the major cider-producing areas of Normandy, where apple trees flank the valleys of the Scie and Varenne rivers. Leave Dieppe southwards on the D915 to le Bois-Robert which offers a panoramic view over the lush Varenne valley. Surrounded by fruit farms — raspberries, strawberries, blackcurrants — you can stop at a 'pick your own' sign, collect a basket and join the throng, or just buy from the numerous roadside sellers.

In May the soft smell of apple blossom hangs heavy throughout the district. The cider apple harvest lasts from September through to December.

Turn westwards on the D107 to Anneville-sur-Scie where guided tours around a cider-makers' are available from June to September.
Take the D3/N27 back to Dieppe.

La Côte d'Albâtre

The Alabaster coast lies between Le Tréport and Le Havre, a distance of about a hundred miles. Tall cliffs, chalk striated with flints and yellow marl, are interrupted at intervals by deep valleys and pockets of shingle sand. Around these beaches resorts have evolved, varying in size, according to the gaps in the cliffs. Behind them lie villages, stretches of beech forests and prosperous farmlands, surrounding large, half-timbered 'Tudor'-looking farmhouses.

Southwards from Dieppe towards Le Havre makes a very pleasant coastal drive, the most picturesque part lying between Senneville and Fécamp. From Dieppe take the D75/D68/D925/D79 to Fécamp.

Resorts before Fécamp are Varengeville-sur-Mer, which is small and set back from the sea in pretty countryside. It has an attractive church (11th-, 13th- and 16th-century) that looks out over the open sea from the cliff top. Georges Braque is buried in its cemetery. Ango Manor (complete with dovecot), built by Jean Ango in 1530, is a quarter of a mile away. Then comes Ste Marguerite, rather similar, and also with an attractive church (12th- to 16th-century), then Quiberville, which boasts a large sandy beach. Veules-les-Roses, lying in a small sheltered valley, is famous for its roses and is as pretty as its name. St Valéry-en-Caux is a pleasant town, with both a fishing port and an important yacht anchorage, and also a safe beach with sand at high tide. It suffered badly in both world wars and the twin limestone buttresses Falaise d'Aval and Falaise d'Amont are both crowned by war memorials. Paluel Nuclear Power Station nearby may be visited. Veulettes-sur-Mer, another comely resort, lies in a wide green hollow by the mouth of the Durdent. Note view from Notre-Dame-du-Salat, a seamen's pilgrimage chapel, and cliffside after Senneville. The road next turns away from the sea and towards Fécamp.

Fécamp

Lunch at L'Escalier, Fécamp.

Fécamp is a dour and functional fishing port — its cod trawlers range as far as Newfoundland. Austere old stone houses climb narrow streets below the cliffs. Its enormous church, first erected by Richard I to house a relic of the holy blood, was once a leading pilgrimage centre, and it has been rebuilt and restored. There is also a Bénédictine museum and distillery for Fécamp was the birthplace of this renowned fiery liqueur. In 1510, the monk Vincelli discovered how to make the liqueur Bénédictine by distilling herbs that grew along the cliffs: he used its restorative powers to heal the sick! The distillery, built in 1892, and museum resemble a Gothic abbey. Some liqueur is still made and sold here. Although the secret recipe was lost during the French Revolution, it was rediscovered in the 19th century by Alexandre Le Grand.

Incidentally, Guy de Maupassant (1850–1893) was born at Fécamp, which often served as a background to his stories. Fécamp is good for an afternoon's exploring, but it is too industrialised a town to spend a holiday at. A point of gastronomic interest: worth tasting are the smoked salmon (producer at Quai Vicomte) and the ubiquitous Bénédictine chocolates.

Étretat

Étretat, 12 miles further on, somewhat Edwardian in style and still elegantly attractive, is set in hilly countryside, between imposing cliffs, Amont and Aval, whose strange-shaped rocks have been compared to elephants plunging their trunks into the sea. The cliffs form porticos, arches and a needle. Indeed the archways gave the town its tourist slogan 'my doors are always open'. It is an exciting and unforgettable sight to watch heavy seas breaking against these lofty sculptured headlands.

Étretat has a tang of the south of France about it and was long a favourite venue of artists such as Corot and Monet, and writers. Guy de Maupassant had a mansion, 'La Guillette', built here. Offenbach (1819–1880) partly composed his 'Tales of Hoffmann' here in 1879.

The town lies behind the beach and promenade, and around an old wooden market place, patriotically used as a hospital during the First World War. Étretat boasts tennis courts, an 18-hole golf course, sailing, horse-riding club and casino (cinema and dancing). When the tide is out quite a bit of sand is exposed, but bathing here is not very good or safe. However, there is a swimming pool, and also some interesting walks to the Falaises d'Aval and d'Amont. Beware, Étretat can be rather expensive.

Dinner and overnight at Hôtel Welcome, Étretat.

L'Escalier
101 Quai Bérigny
76400 Fécamp
Tel: 35 28 26 79

A very reasonable restaurant specialising in fish and classic Norman dishes.

Closed:	27 October to 7 November, and Mondays.
Credit cards:	Visa, Diners Club, Eurocard
Food:	Good Value
Rating:	★★

USEFUL INFORMATION: FÉCAMP

Tourist Office:	Place Bellet Tel: 35 28 20 51
Population:	21,696
Amenities:	Horse riding, sailing, camping, casino.

Specialist producers:
Salmon smokers: 13 Quai Vicomte, 76400 Fécamp, Tel: 35 29 22 86
Bénédictine chocolates: Dumont, 'La Petite Friande', Rue Alex Le Grand.

Hôtel Welcome
Avenue Verdun
Étretat
Tel: 35 27 00 89

A quiet hotel with a garden, yet very central.

Closed:	February and Wednesdays
Rooms:	21
Facilities:	Restaurant, garden, parking
Credit cards:	Eurocard, Visa
Rating:	★★★

L'Éscale
Place Maréchal Foch
Étretat
Tel: 35 27 03 69

Closed:	December and January. Tuesday evenings and Wednesdays
Rooms:	11
Credit cards:	Eurocard, Visa
Rating:	★★★

USEFUL INFORMATION: DIEPPE

Tourist Office:	Boulevard Général de Gaulle
	Tel: 35 84 24 71
Population:	35,360
Amenities:	Golf, shipping port, casino, motor-rail connection.

USEFUL INFORMATION: ÉTRETAT

Tourist Office:	Place Hôtel de Ville (June-Sept.)
	Tel: 35 27 05 21
Population:	1,577
Amenities:	Golf, casino

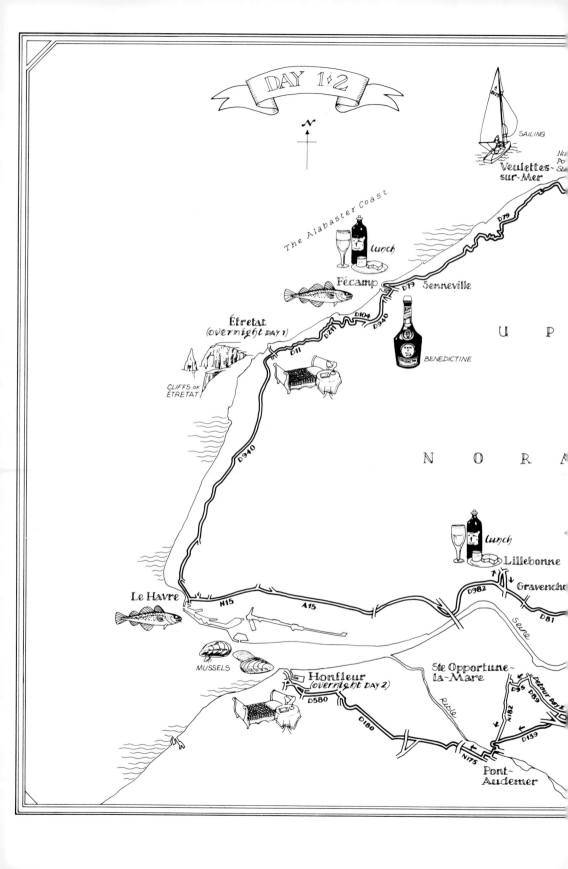

SAILING

St.Marguerite

Quiberville

Dieppe

Varengeville-sur-Mer

D75

Détour Day 1

Valéry-en-Caux

Veules-les-Roses

D68

D925

D79

N27

D915

le Bois-Robert

STRAWBERRIES AND RASPBERRIES

Anneville-sur-Scie

D1017

CIDER AND CALVADOS

Scie

APPLES AND PEARS

E R

FLAX

WHEAT

A N D Y

Caudebec-en-Caux

Rilequier

St.Wandrille

Pont de Brotonne

D490

Détour Day 2

D131

Seine

La Haye-de-Routot

Bourneville

BAKERY

Honfleur

DAY 2

Étretat to Honfleur: approx. 85 miles.

After a morning spent investigating Le Havre, turn inland to lunch at the old Roman town of Lillebonne on the mouth of the Seine. Following the river valley, often termed the 'Route des Abbayes', to St Wandrille, cross the Seine on the Pont de Brotonne to drive through the Forêt de Brotonne, and thence to Honfleur.

Breakfast at Étretat then take the D940 from Étretat to Le Havre.

Le Havre

Le Havre, a transatlantic seaport and industrial centre, completely rebuilt after the last war, is rated a tourist city, and is good for a short visit. Although considered a model of town planning, it is perhaps now too geometrically perfect — horizontal and box-shaped buildings line wide streets laid out like a chess-board — to have any local colour. It includes the residential area of Ste Addresse and the old port of Harfleur.

The port, Le Havre, founded by François I in 1517 to replace nearby Harfleur and Honfleur (on the Côte Fleurie) was named *Le Havre de Grâce* (Haven of Grace) provisionally in 1518 by François. His device, the salamander, was shown on the city's arms. By the end of the 18th century, due to the flourishing West Indian trade and the help given to the Americans during their War of Independence, the town had become an important commercial port and naval station. By the end of the last century, it was France's leading port for the American trade. It was one of the main supply bases for the allied armies during the First World War while in the thirties its liner, *Le Normandie*, was one of the world's most famous passenger ships. However, during the last War, Le Havre had the doubtful honour of being Europe's most badly-damaged port. Allied air-raids combined with German determination to leave nothing of value for the allied armies, resulted in its almost complete destruction. After Le Havre was liberated on 13th September, 1944 (the siege had lasted 11 days), it took two years to finally clear away all the rubble.

Reconstruction took place under the direction of architect, Auguste Perret, and once again it has become one of France's leading ports. Since the opening of the Tancarville Bridge in 1959 (18 miles to the east of Le Havre) the town now has a direct route to the south. Because of its spaciousness, Le Havre is best explored by car; walking around it is rather wearisome.

Starting from the Town Hall, Place de l'Hôtel, take Rue de Paris, a particularly fine shopping street, which leads past Bassin du Commerce and St Joseph's church, an ultra-modern church, one of Auguste Perret's major designs built of reinforced concrete and boasting a 300 ft high belfry. It is especially worth visiting when the morning light streams through its multi-coloured glass panels. At Chaussée Président Kennedy, you can visit the Fine Arts museum (very modernistic in glass and steel), particularly noted for its collection of works by Eugène Boudin (1824-1898), who painted so many of Normandy's beaches, also by Raoul Dufy (1877-1953), both of whom were born here.

You can then drive up Boulevard François I to the magnificent Avenue Foch, which leads back to the Town Hall, or take Boulevard Clemenceau to the Ocean Port and beach beyond.

Above and behind the town is the Montgeon Forest, a recreation area approached through a magnificent road tunnel. From adjoining heights are fine views of the city, harbour and sea. Further westwards lie Le Havre's suburb and resort, Ste Addresse (also called Le Nice Havrais) with its smart Norman-style villas and cottages, and fort.

The Seine, rising in Burgundy and looping its way 480 miles to the sea, resembles an uncoiling snake and is supposed to have acquired its name from the Latin 'Sequana' and Celtic 'Squan' meaning 'to curve'. For centuries, it was the main route to Paris from the coast. Tin traders plied their way along it during the Bronze Age, as eventually did the Romans. It was the road of Caesar, then of Christianity. Later came the pillaging, plundering Vikings and their descendants, the Normans, who constructed many castles and abbeys in its vicinity; so much so that it has been christened the Route des Abbayes. More recent works include the construction of the 15-mile Tancarville canal, a dyke and intensive dredging to make the river more navigable for large merchant ships. Industrialisation of the region (electrical and electronic factories, textile works, paper mills, shipyards and refineries, etc.) have led to the enlargement of its main ports (Rouen and Le Havre) and made Le Havre's outskirts especially sprawling and nondescript.

Follow the A15 out of Le Havre by Tancarville canal, then the D982 to Lillebonne.

Lillebonne

In fact Lillebonne (the Roman Juliobona) is the first place on the Seine after Le Havre to have any character. Juliobona was the rich Gallo–Roman capital of the Calètes tribe — its strategic position enabled it to oversee all river traffic. Unfortunately, this acquired wealth attracted barbarian invaders and led to its eventual downfall. Lillebonne never again reached such prominence.

The ruined Roman theatre, built originally as an amphitheatre in the first century, then turned into a theatre in the 11th century may still be seen. Although much of the stonework was removed for use as building material elsewhere, the scale of the ruins is such that one can still imagine the fights that must have taken place there between gladiators before excited roaring crowds, sometimes numbering as many as 10,000 people. Also noteworthy in Lillebonne is the keep of the castle (rebuilt 12th and 15th centuries) in which William the Conqueror assembled his barons prior to the invasion of England. The castle ruins can be seen easily from the public garden Jean Rostand.

Lunch at Hôtel de la France, Lillebonne.

Following the D81 east past Port-Jérôme and Gravenchon, one returns to industrialisation and petrol refineries. Indeed, it is to the money made from petrol that Gravenchon owes its garden city, built for the petrol workers, and thereby increasing its population from 300 to 8,400.

It is not until the charming village of Villequier, backed by pleasantly wooded country, that the Seine valley dramatically improves. At Villequier there is the Victor Hugo Museum to see — unfortunately his connection with the town is a tragic one. Hugo's favourite daughter, Léopoldine, was drowned here while boating with her husband Charles Vacquerie, just six months after their marriage in 1843. They were killed by the *mascaret*, a tidal wave for which Villequier and Caudebec were renowned, until damming reduced its strength.

Caudebec-en-Caux

Caudebec heralds the beginning of the remarkable Regional Nature Park of the Brotonne, an area of the Seine valley dedicated to the preservation of flora and fauna, and the encouragement and publicising of the old traditional local industries and methods of husbandry. At Caudebec is the Musée de la Marine de Seine, where old-time methods of boat-building and river navigation are demonstrated.

Caudebec-en-Caux, once the capital of the Caux region, is a riverside resort town. Badly-damaged during the war, but carefully restored, it has managed to retain much of its old charm, especially its Flamboyant-Gothic Notre-

Dame church. Two miles to the east, lies St Wandrille, which takes its name from the monastery founded in 649 AD by Count Wandrille from the court of King Dagobert. During the French Revolution, the monks were dispersed and the abbey church allowed to fall into ruins. It was later bought by an English Marquis and in 1894, the Bénédictines returned, but were expelled in 1901. In 1931, the abbey was recovered by the monks, who now sing Gregorian chants and give guided tours. Partly restored, it has great romantic appeal. Worth seeing especially is the 15th-century tithe barn, transported stone by stone from La Neuville du Bosc, 31 miles away, and which has now been turned into a simple monastery church.

Crossing the Seine at Pont de Brotonne (a massive modern toll bridge built on dramatic sweeping lines), a scenic drive through the Forêt de Brotonne (D131) ends at Bourneville. At Bourneville is the Regional Park's Musée des Metiers offering an impressive display of local rural crafts and industries.

Detour

The Regional Park has various other heritage museums in the area. At La Haye-de-Routot (D131/D40) a baker produces delicious 'Pain de Campagne' in his brick ovens; while at Ste Opportune-la-Mare (D89/D95 from Bourneville) the mastersmith explains and demonstrates the workings of his forge. And, at nearby Maison de la Pomme, you will forget about wine made from grapes when you taste the variety of drinks made from apples — Calvados and cider are only two.

From Bourneville go west along the D139 to Pont Audemer, then take the N175/D180 to Honfleur.

Honfleur

Tall, narrow, sometimes half-timbered, slate-roofed houses, restaurants — serving the local speciality, shrimps and cockles — and cafés surround the old port, packed with sailing craft. The 16th-century governor's house — La Lieutenance — guards its entrance. Although Honfleur played an important part in the Hundred Years' War — from time to time it was occupied by the English — its military rôle ended about the end of the 15th century. Its heyday was during the 16th and 17th centuries when trade with America and the East Indies made it an important maritime and commercial port. It was the birthplace of many intrepid seafarers. Samuel Champlain (of Dieppe) set sail from here with a local crew in 1608, a voyage which resulted in the founding of Quebec.

The rise of Le Havre as a seaport brought about Honfleur's decline, but the 19th century brought it a life of a different sort, when many artists came to live here, gathering round Eugène Louis Boudin (1824–1898), precursor of the Impressionists, at the Ferme Saint-Siméon (about a half a mile from the town centre), now an expensive and luxurious hostelry. Monet, Corot, Bonington, Jongkind and Sisley worked here. Some of the works of the Impressionists may be seen in the Musée Eugène Boudin in Place Erik Satie.

Although rather commercialised, it is still fascinating to wander round the old dock; the picturesque quaysides and quaint old cobbled streets behind were once inhabited by rich ship-builders. The old folk museum and 15th-century Ste Catherine church are both worth visiting. Ste Catherine is unique in Normandy — a region of good stone — in that it is built out of wood and was constructed by local ship-builders. It has two naves and the vaulting above resembles an upside-down ship's hull. The bell tower, also of wood, stands apart and opposite the church.

Honfleur lies at the foot of the Côte de Grace, from whose heights — the Calvary, Notre-Dame chapel and Mont Jolie — are viewpoints over the Tancarville bridge and the busy industrial Le Havre roadstead.

Dinner and overnight at La Ferme St. Siméon et son Manoir, Honfleur.

Hôtel de la France
1 rue de la République
76170 Lillebonne
Tel: 35 38 04 88

Although right in the centre of the town you can eat outside under
pretty umbrellas. They are justly proud of their cuisine.

Closed:	Sunday evenings
Rooms:	20
Facilities:	Parking
Credit cards:	American Express, Eurocard, Visa
Rating:	★★

USEFUL INFORMATION: LILLEBONNE

Tourist Office:	4 Rue Pasteur
	Tel: 35 38 51 05
Population:	9,675

La Ferme St Siméon et son Manoir
Route Adolphe-Marais
14600 Honfleur
Tel: 31 89 23 61

One of the Relais and Châteaux group with prices and quality to match.
La Ferme is a seventeenth-century manor house set in beautiful gardens.
It was a favourite gathering place for the early Impressionists when run as
an inn by Mère Toutain. It has been exquisitely renovated by the Boelen
family, the bedrooms are truly luxurious and the food is of top class
quality. An epicurean high spot if you have the money. Otherwise opt for
one of their bargain weekday menus and soak up as much atmosphere as
you can before retiring to a more modest establishment for the night.

La Ferme St Siméon et son Manoir (contd.)

Open:	All year
Rooms:	38
Facilities:	Bar, restaurant, tennis, jacuzzi, gardens
Credit cards:	Visa, Eurocard, Mastercard, Access
Food:	Grand, top class
Rating:	★★★★★

Le Cheval Blanc
Quai Passagers
Honfleur
Tel: 31 89 13 49

Closed:	15 November to 1 March
Rooms:	35
Facilities:	Restaurant
Rating:	★★★

Le Dauphin
10 Place P-Berthelot
Honfleur
Tel: 31 88 15 53

Rating:	★★★

USEFUL INFORMATION: HONFLEUR

Tourist Office:	33 Cours Fosses
	Tel: 31 89 23 30
Population:	8,376
Amenities:	Port, old and new

Ferme Saint-Siméon

La Ferme Saint-Siméon en 1900

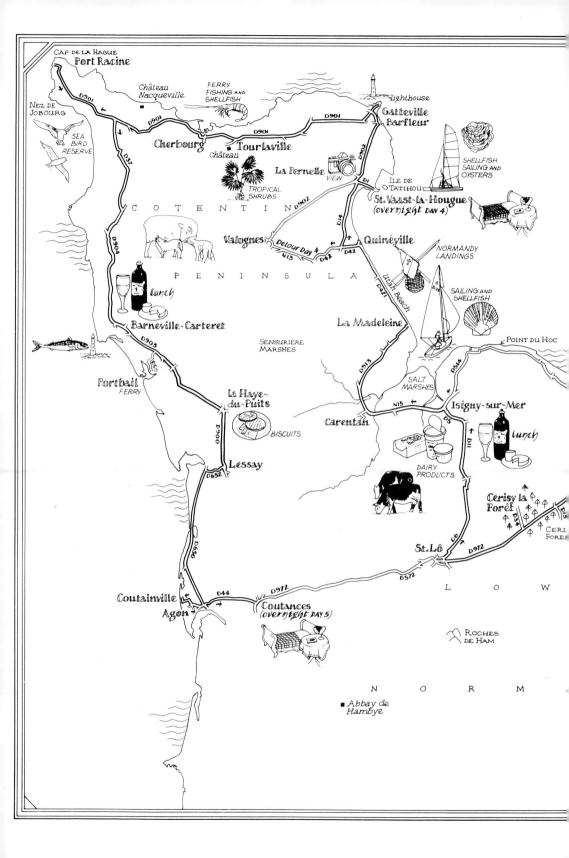

CAP DE LA HAGUE
Port Racine

Château
Nacqueville

FERRY
FISHING AND
SHELLFISH

lighthouse

Gatteville
Barfleur

NEZ DE
JOBOURG

SEA
BIRD
RESERVE

D501

D901

D901

D901

Cherbourg

Tourlaville
château

La Pernelle
VIEW

TROPICAL
SHRUBS

ILE DE
TATIHOU

St. Vaast-la-Hougue
(overnight DAY 4)

SHELLFISH
SAILING AND
OYSTERS

D37

D902

D902

D1

D14

C O T E N T I N

D904

Valognes

Detour Day

N13

D42

D42

Quinéville

NORMANDY
LANDINGS

P E N I N S U L A

lunch

Barneville-Carteret

Utah Beach

La Madeleine

SAILING AND
SHELLFISH

POINT DU HOC

D903

D915

SALT
MARSHES

D514

SENSURIÈRE
MARSHES

D5

Portbail
FERRY

la Haye-
du-Puits

BISCUITS

Carentan

N13

Isigny-sur-Mer

lunch

D900

D900

DAIRY
PRODUCTS

D11

Lessay

D652

Cerisy la
Forêt

D15

D34

CERI
FORES

D650

D6

St. Lô

D972

D572

L O W

Coutainville

Agon

D44

D972

Coutances
(overnight DAY 5)

ROCHES
DE HAM

N O R M

Abbay de
Hambye

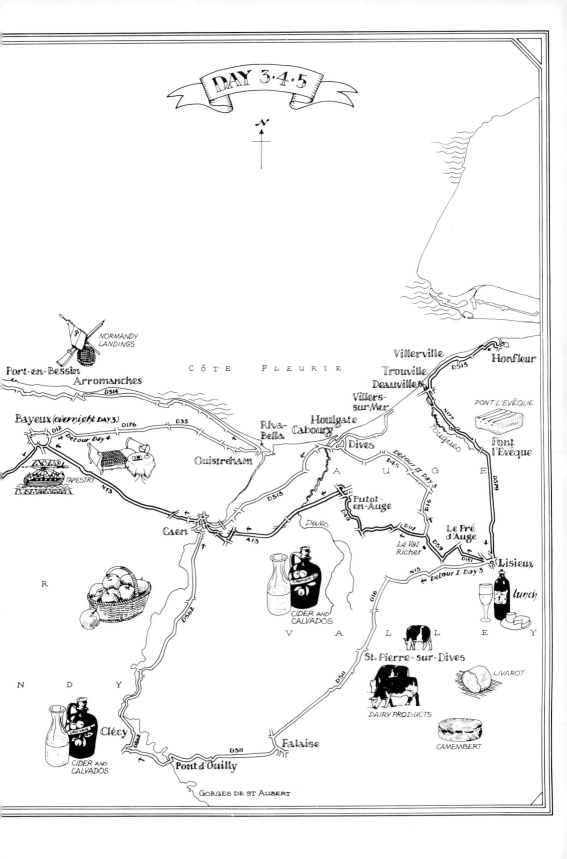

DAY 3·4·5

N

NORMANDY LANDINGS

Port-en-Bessin   Arromanches   CÔTE   FLEURIE   Villerville   Honfleur

Trouville
Deauville

D514   Villers-sur-Mer   PONT L'EVÊQUE

Bayeux (overnight DAY 3)   D176   D35   Riva-Bella   Houlgate   Cabourg   Pont l'Evêque

D12   Detour Day 4   Dives

TAPESTRY   N13   Ouistreham   A   U   G   E   Detour II Day 5

Putot-en-Auge   Le Pré d'Auge

D513   Dives   Le Val Richer   D53   D181   Lisieux

Caen   A13   N15   Detour I Day 5   lunch

R   CIDER AND CALVADOS   V   A   L   L   E   Y

St. Pierre-sur-Dives   LIVAROT

D562   D16

N   D   Y   D511   DAIRY PRODUCTS

Clécy   Falaise   CAMEMBERT

CIDER AND CALVADOS   D511

Pont d'Ouilly

GORGES DE ST AUBERT

Near Lisieux

DAY 3

Honfleur to Bayeux: approx. 78 miles.

Sample the delights of those well-established family resorts of the Côte Fleurie before turning inland at Deauville to reconnoitre the Pays de l'Auge — a land of cheese and cider. After lunching at the pilgrimage centre of Lisieux, you will have to choose your route, depending on the time at your disposal. The main route meanders through the Calvados and cider-producing heart of Pays de l'Auge and then on to an afternoon exploring William the Conqueror's city, Caen, before arriving for supper at your hotel in Bayeux.

Alternatively, from Lisieux you may choose instead to return to the Côte Fleurie and follow a coastline of resorts famed for their vast sandy beaches. A further option takes you south into the Suisse Normande to Falaise, William the Conqueror's birthplace, before rejoining the main route at Caen.

Travels in Normandy

Breakfast at Honfleur.

The Côte Fleurie

Honfleur lies at the eastern end of the Côte Fleurie, the most popular part of Normandy's long coastline, which lies between the Seine and Dives rivers. It is a magnificent stretch of wide sandy beaches, backed by a hinterland of low-lying hills — a pretty countryside of hedge-bound meadows, neat orchards of apple trees, farmsteads and stone cottages. This coastline, gentler than that of the Alabaster coast, north of the Seine, was once the preserve of the wealthy and cosmopolitan. Today it attracts a different type of holidaymaker. Expensive exclusive hotels are being replaced by villas, rented apartments, camp sites and second homes.

After Honfleur comes the often pretty and occasionally dramatic Normandy Corniche, a road running along hills beside the sea, which meets the coast again at Villerville, a lively resort. The corniche ends at Trouville. This is where the splendid stretch of sand starts. Resorts Trouville-Deauville lie either side of the Touques river, and are linked by ferry boat and bridge.

Trouville, less smart then Deauville, and lying at the foot of wooded hills, is the Côte's most popular resort. Unlike Deauville, it is geared to commerce as well as holidays, and can be visited at any time of the year. It is a good tourist centre — from here buses do tours of Normandy and also go to Brittany (July to September). Trouville, the older resort, was a favourite sojourn of the Empress Eugénie and many of Trouville's older villas recall the era of the Second Empire.

Deauville, originally an extension for the rich of Trouville, now with its smart hotels and entertainments — casinos, horse-racing, regattas, tournaments, galas, golf, polo and yacht basin — is the Cannes and Monte Carlo of the Côte Fleurie. Its season starts in July and ends on the fourth Sunday in August with the *Grand Prix*. The *Planches*, a wooden plank promenade running the length of Deauville's and Trouville's beautiful sandy beaches, is backed by terraces, flower gardens and elegant buildings. A leisurely stroll along the fashionable boardwork, perhaps stopping for coffee at a beachside cafe, is the best way to absorb the flavour of this international up-market resort.

For a contrast of scenery turn south on the N177 and D579 along the Touques valley and drive into the heart of the Pays de l'Auge. The Pays de l'Auge, crisscrossed with streams (known locally as *Douets*), green meadows and cider orchards, is one of the most fertile regions in France. For local interest look out for the cattle fairs, also the cafés surrounding the market places, where cattle owners, dealers and agents do business over an aperitif. Because of its reputation for dairy products, the Pays de l'Auge attracts cheese connoisseurs from far and wide.

Pont l'Évêque.

Pont l'Évêque claims to be the producer of France's oldest cheese. In the 13th century it was known as Angelot. Today's Pont l'Éveque can trace its origin as far back as the 17th century. It is so widely on offer in the town that you will probably be unable to avoid having at least one nibble of this famous cheese. As Pont l'Évêque is firmly in the Calvados region, it boasts a Calvados museum. Also to note here is the Flamboyant-Gothic St Michael's church, flanked by a square tower and the former convent of the Dominican sisters of the island at the end of the Place du Palais de Justice. Pont l'Évêque was badly damaged during World War Two.

Lisieux

Lisieux's massive 'Roman Byzantine' church (started in 1923) presents an unexpected reminder of the east as its dome rises ethereally above trees on a hilltop. Dedicated to Ste Thérèse, it is an important place of pilgrimage — 15th August, last Sunday in September, 30th September and 3rd October.

Ste Thérèse (The Little Flower), a delicate girl, entered a convent when she was 15, and died in 1897 at the age of 24. She wrote the *Histoire d'un âme* (story of a soul), an account of her life in which she defined the 'little way' a naive yet heroic way in which anyone could lead a Christian life. Her booklet became very popular after her death, many people believed that her spirit could cure sickness. In 1925 Pope Pius XI canonised Thérèse, calling her 'the star' of his pontificate.

Lisieux's 12th- to 13th-century cathedral, St Pierre (badly-damaged in the war but restored), has an extremely elegant transept. Its huge central chapel was remodelled in the Flamoyant-Gothic style by order of Pierre Cauchon, Bishop of Lisieux, who played such an important role in the trial of Joan of Arc. It was here that Thérèse Martin attended Mass.

Although Lisieux is the largest industrialised and agricultural centre in Pays de l'Auge, it has its picturesque side: the half-timbered houses of the Rue Henri-Chéron and the 17th-century episcopal palace, which possesses a magnificent leather-lined chamber and a fine staircase. Thomas-à-Becket spent much of his exile in Lisieux and Henry II married Eleanor of Aquitaine here. The town's long history is well-illustrated in the Musée du Vieux Lisieux.

Lunch at L'Auberge du Pêcheur, Lisieux.

Situated in a valley where the Touques, Orbiquet and Cirieux meet, and at a junction of roads, Lisieux makes a good stopping place. There are plenty of hotels, but beware of coming during an important pilgrimage. It lies in a picturesque area of manor houses, abbeys and old villages, and makes a good centre for tours, especially into the Suisse Normande.

Suisse Normande

Suisse Normande is certainly not Switzerland — there are no lakes or high mountains. Nevertheless, the Orne river, curling through the Amorican Massif, has carved this area into a region of deep gorges, valleys and high cliffs. From peaks such as Roc d'Oëtre and Pain de Sucre, there are some splendid views of the rolling countryside. Clècy, a large picturesque village, (possesses a folklore museum, cider cellar and is a good starting place for hillside walks, rock-climbing, fishing and canoeing) curving around the Orne, lies at its centre.

Most of Suisse Normande lies in Calvados, and its nearest large town is Falaise, 16 miles from Pont d'Ouilly, where the Orne and Noireau rivers meet — a tourist crossroads of the region.

Detour I

Rather than continuing toward Caen, if you have any extra time this would be a good opportunity to travel further south into the region of Suisse Normande.

From Lisieux take the N13/D16/D511 to Falaise via St Pierre-sur-Dives, a pleasant country town which evolved around an 11th-century Bénédictine abbey, of which little remains. The monks also built its low, timbered market hall, where following time-honoured tradition the locals display their rich, creamy butter, eggs, cheeses and poultry in large wicker baskets. After a visit here your journey may be slowed down when you find yourself driving behind a horse-drawn, covered cart as the marketeers return through the winding lanes to their distant farms. St Pierre's fine abbey church is worth a visit. The town's history may be seen illustrated in the three modern stained-glass windows. A new museum showing cheese-making will open in June 1988.

Falaise, set in the Ante valley, a ravine scattered with rocky spurs, has many links with England. Its old castle, birthplace of William the Conqueror, is still a great sight, aloft on its crag, looking almost as impressive, I'm sure, as ever it did in medieval times. Of the castle, constructed in the 10th century, there remains only its great 12th-century keep and 15th-century Talbot tower and ramparts. Innumerable battles have been fought over it, the last but certainly not least being during the Second World War — the Talbot tower was used by the Germans to fire down onto Montgomery's troops, advancing along the Caen road. Take the panoramic road at the foot of the castle which passes the medieval wash-house, rounded towers and Cordeliers' Gate.

Duke Robert (William's father) is supposed to have first seen the high-spirited Arlette (William's mother), the tanner's daughter, washing clothes in the rill below the castle. The memorial to this legendary event, along with the now neatly-enclosed gushing Ante, has been incorporated into the valley and gardens which have replaced the quaint old tanneries and cottages. No doubt, William spent some of his childhood playing amongst this valley's craggy rocks.

Continue on the D511 through Pont d'Ouilly (where you can turn south to explore the gorges), then the D562 to Clécy. Here you may visit a cider cellar or maybe take a pedalo along the river, continue north to Caen.

To experience the charm of the Pays de l'Auge, leave Lisieux on the D151 to Pré d'Auge. Nearby (D59) stands the ancient abbey of le Val Richer.

This region is part of a tourist circuit known as the Cider Route, which links the towns of Cambremer, Beuvron, Beaufour and Bonnebosq. Along the lanes are signposts marked 'Route de Cidre' with an apple symbol. Annually a number of farmhouses along the route are selected to display the 'Cru de Cambremer' sign — these farms are open to the public. You can visit the cellars, taste and buy their cider and Calvados, secure in the knowledge that all is of a guaranteed standard. Frequently you will come across Pommeau on offer — this is a traditional Normandy aperitif made from a combination of cider must and Calvados.

Drive slowly through sleepy villages and hamlets to Putot-en-Auge (with a noteworthy church and manor house) and thence along the autoroute to Caen.

Detour II

After le Val Richer you may prefer to return to the Côte Fleurie (D45) and make your way along the coastal route to Caen. After Trouville-Deauville comes one resort after another, all rather alike, and overlooking vast plateaux of sand. There is Bénerville and Blonville, merging at the foot of Mont Canisy, and Villers-sur-mer, quite elegant, and separated from Houlgate, next, by the Vaches Noires cliff.

Houlgate, an attractive relaxed leafy town set in the Drochon valley makes a good choice for a family holiday. Between it and Dives are some of this coast's best panoramic views — the Dives Valley, Dives-Cabourg town, and the coast either side of the mouth of the Orne.

Like Trouville-Deauville, Dives, a small industrial town, faces its neighbour, Cabourg, across the River Dives. Dives will be remembered as the port from which William the Conqueror set off with his fleet in 1066 to conquer England. He landed at Pevensey on 28th September: on Christmas Day, he was crowned at Westminster Abbey. On the west wall of our Lady of Dives (mainly 14th- and 15th-century, built onto an 11th-century church) you can see a list of his barons and the companions-in-arms who sailed with him.

Cabourg, originally a fisherman's village, was created during the era of the Second Empire like Trouville. It was built symmetrically in the shape of a fan, with the casino and Grand Hotel as the focal point from which shady avenues radiate. The Boulevard Marcel Proust, a magnificent promenade, runs beside its fine sandy beach. French literature owes its description of 19th-century Normandy beach life to Proust's stay in this resort. From Cabourg, you can drive direct to Caen, or you can continue along the coast road from Le Hôme and Merville-Franceville then cross Caen canal, and continue on to the city.

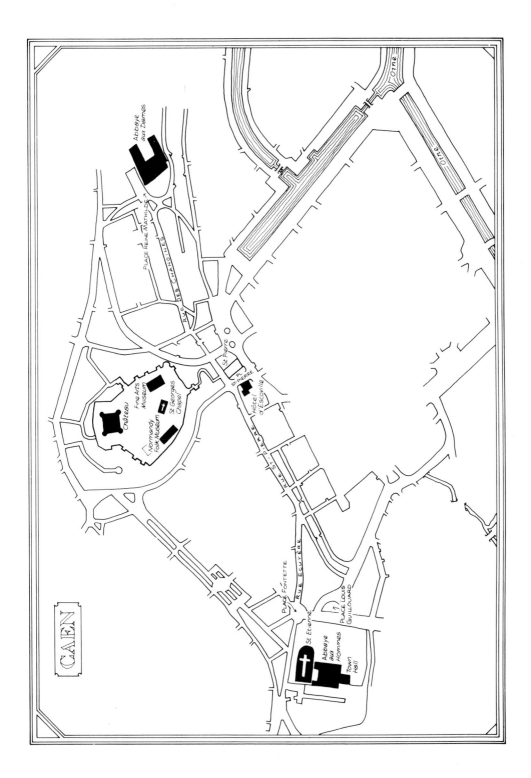

Caen

Caen, capital of Lower Normandy and Normandy's most important industrial city is also the centre of a rich agricultural region. Although three-quarters of the town was destroyed in 1944 during the battle of Normandy, earning Caen the title 'Anvil of Victory', nevertheless, phoenix-like, a magnificent and well-planned city has arisen from the ashes. Caen is surrounded by good stone quarries, incidentally, they supplied stone for some of our finest English buildings — notably the White Tower in the Tower of London. Reconstruction was carried out swiftly and carefully. Many narrow streets were eliminated and replaced by broad thoroughfares, while the better streets were restored to their original aspect. Fortunately, the abbeys and churches were spared, while Caen's old castle could even be said to have been visually improved, it now stands out boldly, as it must have done originally, without being spoiled by the sight of clustering buildings.

Caen, standing on an island at the confluence of the Orne and Odon, was early fortified by the Vikings. It took on new importance when Duke William built a castle in this, his favourite city, in the 11th century. After subduing rebel barons, he felt sufficiently established in his duchy to ask for the hand in marriage of his cousin, Mathilda. The union was opposed by Pope Leo IX, who disapproved of cousins' marrying. In penance and to help gain the Pope's support, William and Mathilda founded two abbeys — Abbaye aux Hommes and Abbaye aux Dames — and some hospitals and churches. Mathilda acted as regent of Normandy while William was in England. She was created Queen of England in 1068, but was buried in her Abbaye aux Dames.

Caen was occupied by the English during the Hundred Years' War, it was a centre of Protestantism during the Wars of Religion, and the centre of Norman federalism during the French Revolution. Charlotte Corday (1768–1793), assassin of the notorious revolutionary Jean Paul Marat, came from Caen. During the two months' battering (bombs *and* shells) of the Second World War, the townspeople sought refuge in cellars and in the crypts of old churches. Some sheltered in the Fleury quarries half a mile from the town.

For a tour of Caen, start outside the Syndicat d'Initiative in Hôtel d'Escoville, built by a rich 16th-century merchant, in Place St Pierre. Nearby is Caen's famous castle, impressive although now a mere shell, standing boldly alone on the hill. You can stroll through its park and visit St Georges chapel (12th- to 15th-century, a memorial to all those killed fighting for Normandy), the Fine Arts museum, and the Normandy Folk museum. Near here, too, is the mostly Gothic church of St Pierre (some exhuberant renaissance decorations inside), richly endowed by Caen's wealthy merchants. Its belfry, erected in 1308, was destroyed in 1944 when hit by a shell from HMS Rodney during the battle of Caen. It has been restored.

Rue St Pierre leads into Rue Ecuyère and Place Fontette. Nearby in Place Louis Guillouard is the Town Hall (it has some magnificent woodwork inside), which was once the abbey buildings of Aux Hommes. This and St Etienne church are best seen as an ensemble from Place Louis Guillouard. St Etienne, tall and cool with beautiful sweeping lines is very superior architecturally. Although extensively restored, nothing can detract from its magnificent outline. William the Conqueror was buried here, near the altar, but his remains were thrown into the river during the Revolution.

Abbaye aux Dames is some distance away on the other side of the castle, approached down Rue des Chanoines, which leads into Place Reine Mathilde. Its ensemble is not so beautiful as Aux Hommes. It appears squat, due perhaps to the fact that its spires were destroyed during the Hundred Years' War. Its abbey was also more seriously damaged during the last war. The tomb of Queen Mathilda is in the chancel of its Holy Trinity church, which has a large crypt, dedicated to St Nicholas. Fortunately this has been very well-preserved (note the carvings on the capitals).

Take the N13 to Bayeux.

Dinner and overnight at Hôtel Luxembourg, Bayeux.

Auberge du Pêcheur
2 bis Rue de Verdun
14100 Lisieux
Tel: 31 31 16 85

Closed:	1 September to 1 November, Sunday evenings and Mondays
Credit cards:	Visa
Food:	Fish and seafood a speciality
Rating:	★★

USEFUL INFORMATION: LISIEUX

Tourist Office:	11 Rue Alençon
	Tel: 31 62 08 41
Population:	25,998

Hôtel Luxembourg
25 Rue Bouchers
Bayeux
Tel: 31 92 00 04

Situated right in the centre of town.

Rooms:	24
Facilities:	Restaurant, car park
Credit cards:	Visa, Diners Club, Am.Ex.
Rating:	★★★

Hôtel Pacary
117 Rue St Patrice
Bayeux
Tel: 31 92 16 11

Rooms:	65
Facilities:	Restaurant, swimming pool, car park
Credit cards:	Visa
Rating:	★★★

USEFUL INFORMATION: BAYEUX

Tourist Office:	1 Rue Cuisiniers
	Tel: 31 92 16 26
Population:	15,237
Amenities:	Cathedral and, of course, the Tapestry

USEFUL INFORMATION: CAEN

Tourist Office:	Place St Pierre
	Tel: 31 86 27 65
Population:	117,119
Amenities:	Churches, museums

USEFUL INFORMATION: FALAISE

Tourist Office:	32 Rue G. Clemenceau
Population:	8,820

Rue St. Martin, Bayeux

DAY 4

Bayeux to St Vaast-la-Hougue: approx. 74 miles.

After exploring the picturesque streets of Bayeux our route turns inland to St Lô — centre of the region — thence northwards to lunch at Isigny. Alternatively you could follow the coastal resorts from bustling Ouistreham to Isigny on the salt marshes.

Setting off along the Cotentin Peninsula, where the beaches are living landmarks of the 1944 invasions, the route takes in Utah beach and north to St Vaast-la-Hougue. A detour inland to Valognes — butter is the chief product of this market town — will enable you to see its remaining 18th-century houses; this offers just a glimpse of its past splendours, for so much was destroyed in World War Two.

Breakfast at Bayeux.

Bayeux

Bayeux, old capital of the Bessin region, has the distinction of being the first town in France to be liberated on 7th June, 1944, after the Normandy landings. And, miraculously, it suffered little damage. So, it remains as it was, narrow streets lined with picturesque old houses, stone bridges, and its chief treasures — the Tapestry, cathedral and museum — all intact.

Bayeux might be called the cradle of the Norman dukes, for it was here that Rollo of St Clair-sur-Epte fame married Popa, daughter of Count Béranger, its governor. In 905, their son known as William Longsword and great-great-grandfather of William the Conqueror, was born.

The first thing to see at Bayeux is, of course, the celebrated Tapestry, which since 1983 is housed in the Centre Guillaume le Conquérant in the Rue de Nesmond. The exhibition is now displayed in a rather gimmicky fashion. One is first exposed to the feeling that one is part of an invading force, induced by pictures of boats and sound-effects of flapping sails, then explanatory maps of invasion and background information, before seeing the actual Tapestry housed in airtight showcases. It is captioned in Latin but you can hire an earphone which relays a commentary in English about it.

The Tapestry, 231 ft by 19½ inches is, in fact, an embroidery of coloured wool on linen, containing 58 scenes of restrained colouring. Its origin is not conclusively known, but most probably it was made in England by a school of Saxon embroiderers, and it is certainly highly improbable that the Queen Mathilda made it, which was once believed, and which is why it was called *La Tapisserie de la Reine*.

It is a fascinating piece of work, showing as it does, William's side of the conquest: his meeting with Harold, who swore his ill-fated oath at Bayeux to let William be king of England, the preparations for the conquest, the battle, the victory. The English, the 'baddies' can be identified by their drooping moustaches, the Normans, the 'goodies', by their close-cropped hair. Most probably it was intended to be hung round the nave of Bayeux cathedral, as a simple explanation of what had taken place, or a piece of propaganda for the people. The Tapestry exhibition is open daily throughout the year.

The cathedral, built on the site of an ancient Gallo-Roman temple was consecrated in 1077 by Bishop Odo, William's turbulent half brother. Although an imposing Norman Gothic cathedral, it is not one of Normandy's best. It was restored about 1150 by Philip of Harcourt, after having been badly damaged by Henry I in 1105, and enriched with carvings. Note the story of Thomas-à-Becket's martyrdom on the south transept doorway tympanum.

Not far from here is the Baron Gérard museum, which has an art collection, pottery, Bayeux porcelain, and dolls (illustrating the court of Louis XIV) and a collection of lace and tapestry. In the 19th century Bayeux lacemaking was reckoned among the finest in Europe.

Leave Bayeux by the D572/972 through the forest of Cerisy to St Lô.

St Lô

One's first sight of St Lô is of its 'Enclos', a vast rocky wall up a hillside, surrounding the old town, and above which peep tops of houses and Notre-Dame church.

St Lô was an old Roman town, a fortress in medieval times, a centre of the weaving industry, and a Protestant stronghold during the Wars of Religion. It was also a key road communication centre in the Battle of Normandy, a pivot of German resistance. When it fell on 19th July, 1944, the town had been so badly battered that it was named 'capital of the ruins'.

To some extent, the extensive damage did some good in that it clarified the outline of the old ramparts, giving the town a more distinct and individual character. To see there now is the church of Our Lady (13th- to 17th-century), the Fine Arts museum (16th-century tapestries and 19th-century French paintings), and the Horses' Stud (mostly English and French thoroughbreds selected for the breeding of race horses) which you will pass on the Bayeux road. Places to visit nearby are the Roches de Ham (2 miles south of Condé-sur-Vire), a magnificent escarpment of rocks with a good view along the Vire valley; and the Abbaye de Hambye (to the southwest, D999/13), whose majestic peaceful 12th-century ruins are situated in the secluded Sienne valley. There are guided tours. The Conventual buildings may be visited.

From St Lô take the D6/11/5 north to Isigny-sur-Mer for lunch before embarking upon the Manche.

Detour from Bayeux

Instead of visiting St Lô you may prefer to drive along the Calvados coast to rejoin the main route for lunch at Isigny. Take the D12/D35/76 to Ouistreham.

The Calvados coast lies between the Orne and Vire rivers. Calvados is supposed to be a corruption of 'Salvador', the name of a ship of the Spanish Armada, which ran aground on the underwater rocks near Arromanches. Here, long stretches of flat sandy beaches, interspersed with sand dunes and salt marshes, edge an undulating, not very interesting countryside. Over recent years the resorts along this more evocatively renamed Côte Nacre (mother-of-pearl coast) have become popular with campers.

The long flat beaches served a grimmer purpose in June 1944 when they formed the bridgehead of the toehold of the allied attack to liberate France and Europe from the Nazi régime. Mementoes of the fighting — pill-boxes, gun-batteries, barbed wire and the occasional land mine — still litter these invasion beaches. More permanent reminders are the cemeteries, memorials and museums. The best-known museum is the Mulberry (artificial port used up to the end of August 1944) and War Museum at Arromanches (showing royal naval films of landings, diaramas, models, photographs and collections of war equipment).

The largest and most popular resort along this stretch of coast is Ouistreham-Riva-Bella, Caen's ancient port and once often used by the English in their forays against the city. Today it is a busy international yachting centre, famous for its oysters and seaweed (which imparts a healthy tang to the air when exposed at low tide). It also has a landing museum. Lively Port-en-Bessin, known locally as 'Port', tucked in between high cliffs, is both busy and picturesque. From here you can see the American Utah and Omaha beaches and a large American war cemetery at St Laurent-sur-Mer. The Point du Hoc offers a splendid view of the Cotentin Peninsula before turning inland to Isigny.

Lunch at Hôtel du Commerce, Isigny-sur-Mer.

Surrounded by salt marshes (try the *agneau pré-salé*). Isigny is sited near the mouth of the Vire. The fishing boats bobbing at the quayside hold baskets filled with a wonderful variety of oysters and shellfish.

The Manche, or Cotentin Peninsula

When looking at a map of France, one's first impression of Normandy is of its Cotentin Peninsula, jutting out to sea like a raised arm, or merely its sleeve. Hence the word *manche* (sleeve), which has given its name to the department, and indeed to the surrounding channel. The Cotentin, a wild austere region, is separated from the Bocage (a pretty area of orchards and meadows, surrounded by tall hedges and woodland), by a depression, which is flooded over at certain times of the year.

This region was once very poor and many Normans emigrated from here in the 11th and 12th centuries, to Britain, the Holy Land and Sicily, then later to the New World. The people remaining developed small-scale industries, such as weaving and copperware, and more recently, cattle-breeding, horses (around Ste Mère-Église), and dairy-farming. The Manche is still very much a region of scattered farmsteads and hamlets, rather than villages, and small market towns but it is becoming increasingly popular with holidaymakers, especially campers.

The eastern side of the Cotentin peninsula played a vital part in the Normandy landings of the last war, when American airborne troops were landed at Ste Mère-Église and along the Utah beach. The plan was to cut the Cotentin in two and seize Cherbourg. However the resulting war of the hedgerows came as an unpleasant surprise, for it was a terrain easier to defend than to advance through, especially in Centurion tanks. Casualties were high. Barneville, on the Cotentin's west side was captured on 18th June, and finally, Cherbourg on the 26th June.

Take the N13 to Carentan — dairy-farming centre and gateway to the Cotentin. There is an important market held here every Monday. To note are the 15th-century arcades and the remains of an old covered market and 14th-century Notre-Dame. More recent is the new yacht harbour. A canal leads from here to the Bay of Vey.

Continue north (N13/D913) to la Madeleine from where the vast expanse of Utah beach stretches out before you. Monuments and memorials underline the extent of the allied troop movements. At Quinéville, beyond the sand dunes and yacht harbour looms, surprisingly, a grand Château, now used as an hotel. King James II stayed here, it is said, while his Irish and French allies fought for him against the English off St Vaast-la-Hougue.

Detour

Inland lies Valognes, sometimes known as the Versailles of Normandy. Not all its 18th-century grandeur was destroyed in the war — Hôtel de Beaumont still shows some of its original splendour. In the lodge of the Grand Quartier there is an instructive regional cider museum, and a museum of brandy in the Hôtel de Thieuville.

St Vaast-la-Hougue

St Vaast-la-Hougue is a small fishing port (important as an oyster-breeding centre and specialising in shellfish) that possesses a magnificent stretch of water for sailing. In olden times, St Vaast was used as a landing place for British armies. King Stephen landed here in 1137: two centuries later came Edward III, Henry V and Henry VI. More important, in 1692, an Anglo-Dutch fleet defeated the French navy in nearby waters (Louis XIV supported James II; deposed by William of Orange in 1688) thus frustrating James II's hopes of invading England and regaining his throne.

St Vaast is being modernised quickly. A new marina and yacht club have been built to take advantage of the near-perfect sailing conditions here. But its small fishing village and picturesque 17th-century fishing port still remain from the past. At low tide, the Ile de Tatihou can be reached on foot (take your wellies as it is usually muddy). To see in particular are the oyster farms at Le Vauban (open to the public) and a splendid view over the region from the top of La Pernelle.

Dinner and overnight at Hôtel Restaurant France at Fuschias, St Vaast.

```
┌─────────────────────────────────────────────────────────┐
│ USEFUL INFORMATION: ST LÔ                               │
│ Tourist Office:        2 Rue Havin                      │
│                        Tel: 33 05 02 09                 │
│ Population:            24,792                            │
└─────────────────────────────────────────────────────────┘
```

```
┌─────────────────────────────────────────────────────────┐
│ USEFUL INFORMATION: VALOGNES                            │
│ Tourist Office:        Place Château (10 May-Sept.)     │
│                        Tel: 33 40 11 55                 │
│ Population:            6,963                             │
└─────────────────────────────────────────────────────────┘
```

Hôtel du Commerce
5 Rue E. Demagny
14230 Isigny-sur-Mer
Tel: 31 22 01 44

A very charming and exuberantly decorated place. The prices are reasonable and the food good. Many regional dishes such as Escalope Normande, Tripes à la mode de Caen.

Closed:	January and February. Restaurant closed Sunday evenings and Mondays except in July and August.
Rooms:	10
Credit cards:	Carte Bleu, Mastercard
Food:	Reasonable and simple
Rating:	★★

Hôtel Restaurant France et Fuchsias
18 Rue Maréchal-Foch
50550 St Vaast-la-Hougue
Tel: 33 54 42 26

Bright red fuschias cover the walls of this family-run hotel, spilling through into the conservatory dining room. Very prettily decorated with a lovely secluded garden, the restaurant prides itself on its fresh produce grown at its own farm at Quettehou nearby.

Closed:	3 January to 1 March. Restaurant closed Monday and Tuesday lunchtime in Winter.
Rooms:	32
Facilities:	Restaurant, garden
Credit cards:	Diners Club, Visa, Mastercard, Eurocard
Food:	Lots of fresh fruit and vegetables as well as the usual seafood. Specialities include le navarrin de lotte aux petits légumes.
Rating:	★★

USEFUL INFORMATION: ST VAAST-LA-HOUGUE

Tourist Office:	Quai Vauban (15 June-15 Sept.) Tel: 33 54 41 37
Population:	2,359
Amenities:	Golf

Hôtel Haut Gallion
Route Cherbourg
50700 Valognes
Tel: 33 40 40 00

Closed:	19th December to 3rd January, and Wednesday evenings
Rooms:	40
Credit cards:	American Express, Visa, Eurocard
Rating:	★★★★

The Alabaster Coast

DAY 5

St Vaast-la-Hougue to Coutances: approx. 115 miles.

The morning can be spent exploring the windswept northern tip of the Cotentin Peninsula which has some of the most spectacular scenery in Normandy, perhaps in France. The bustling port of Cherbourg is in stark contrast with the isolated surrounds of Gatteville lighthouse on one side and the rocky wind-blasted tip of La Hague on the other. The circumnavigation of the peninsula continues as we travel down the western side to stop at the fishing port and seaside resort of Barneville-Carteret for lunch. Spare time in the afternoon for a visit to the graceful Romanesque abbey of Lessay before an overnight stop at Coutances.

Breakfast at St Vaast-la-Hougue.

Leave St Vaast by the D1/D902.

On the north-eastern tip of the Cotentin peninsula lies Barfleur port and seaside resort, not beautiful, but it has a certain charm. During medieval times, it was the chief sealink between England and Normandy. It is now famous for its lobster pots.

The road to the lighthouse at pretty Gatteville village, 2 miles away, runs through windswept Breton-type countryside. The lighthouse (200 ft high), is one of the tallest in France. It was on the Quilleboeuf reef not far from the harbour that the ship Blanche Nez, carrying William, only legitimate son of Henry I, to England, foundered in 1120, drowning the heir to the English throne along with 300 other men and women.

Take the D10/D901 west to Cherbourg. The route passes Tourlaville, a Renaissance château surrounded by a picturesque park of tropical shrubs.

Cherbourg

Cherbourg, Normandy's third main port, and the Manche's chief town lies at the mouth of the Divette river and is overlooked by the steep Montagne du Roule. Cherbourg has been used as a port since the Bronze Age when traders left from there for the British Isles.

In spite of its long history, Cherbourg's development as a major port came later than others of similar size because its north side was exposed to high seas. Any breakwaters built there were soon swept away. It was not until 1853 that the planned naval base was finally opened by Napoléon III. Since then, Cherbourg has developed into a passenger port for channel and transatlantic passenger ships. Although it is also an industrial and market town, most of its activities are connected with the port, such as ship repairs and cargo traffic, naval base and garrison, and fishing and sailing. It is at Cherbourg that France builds her atomic submarines.

If you have time to spare at Cherbourg ascend the road to the top of Roule Hill (the main point of German resistance) which will give you a good view over the roadstead and harbour. Nearby is the war and liberation museum. Fairly near at hand lies the Château of Nacqueville (16th-century), most romantic with ivy-covered postern and towers, set in a park of oak trees.

On the other side of Cherbourg the D901 takes you to that flat, wind-torn spur or rock, La Hague. Treeless and bleak, grazed over by sheep and crisscrossed by stone walls, it possesses a sort of wild beauty. A lighthouse stands on an outlying rocky island to warn shipping of this dangerous coast. On the north side lies Port Racine, the smallest port in France. Grandiose and spectacular, enclosed by reefs, Nez de Jobourg is a large rugged promonotory inhabited by a seabird reserve. The landscape is now somewhat marred by the presence of the Usine Atomique de la Hague, an ugly nuclear reprocessing plant, occupying what was once heathland and moor.

The Cotentin's west coast is a succession of large sandy beaches (especially when the tide is out) and smallish rather plain resorts. From Beaumont to the seaside town of Barneville is a picturesque drive (D37/D904) with many good views of the sea and Channel Islands beyond.

Lunch at Les Isles, right on the beach at Barneville-Carteret.

Barneville-Carteret, either side of the Gerfleur estuary, a fishing village resort, has a magnificent rocky headland. It is really three places in one — Carteret is a lively little resort and port with lighthouse and small beach; Barneville Plage, a seafront boulevard, is more staid and residential, while Barneville is the old market town (note its 11th-century church with its 15th-century tower — beautiful decorations on Romanesque arches) also the monument commemorating the cutting of the Cotentin Peninsula (8th June 1944). White sandy beaches stretch southwards for over two miles.

Continue south on the D903 (bear right at La Picauderie on to D50) to Portbail, a shady village with modest grey stone port from which there are regular ferry services to Jersey and Guernsey. Hence the town's tag 'gateway to the isles'. To see here are the 10th-century church of Notre-Dame with 15th-century fortified tower (note 16th-century capitals) and a Gallo-Roman baptistry not far from the church.

Inland a bit lies La Haye-du-Puits, on the edge of the Sensurière marshes. As the town's speciality is Biscuiterie this is an ideal place to stop for afternoon tea. On Wednesdays, the town is taken over by a large and fascinating market.

Lessay

Continue south on the D900 to Lessay to visit the magnificently restored Bénédictine abbey church there. Founded in 1056 by the barons of La Haye-du-Puits, it was badly damaged in 1944, but was magnificently restored using the shattered mellow golden stone. The result is quite beautiful — almost stunningly so — and certainly uplifting when one walks between the nave's massive stone pillars. It is all a wonderful blend of proportions, colour and light plus a mystical indefinable something.

Lessay is also renowned for smoked hams which you can watch being prepared in the traditional way (over wood fires) at the *Jambons du Cotentin*. In the first week in September Lessay hosts its 1000-year-old Fête of the Holy Cross.

Follow the D652/650 to Agon-Coutainville. Coutainville, built amongst the sand dunes, combines with neighbouring Agon to make one of the best-equipped resorts on the west coast — casino, theatre, racecourse, swimming pools, water-skiing, scuba-diving, tennis, horse-riding, cycling and fishing. The vast beaches of this popular family resort are dotted with South Sea island-type straw huts. The surrounding countryside is pretty.

Coutances

Coutances lies about 8 miles inland from Coutainville. Built on the spur of a hill, it is dominated by a splendid soaring Gothic cathedral, which fortunately escaped the war damage done to the surrounding town. The square in front of it, Place du Parvis, has been rebuilt in such a way as to only enhance its beauty.

Coutances, named after a Roman emperor, was a favourite sojourn of the Normans. Geoffrey de Montbray, an early Bishop of Coutances, started on the cathedral's construction in 1056. Although the town was burned down in 1218, a new cathedral was mounted on the remains of the last, a difficult task demanding considerable skill. Inside, dominating the transept, is the octagonal lead-covered lantern tower, 135 ft high, and one of the finest examples of its kind in Normandy. To see also are the churches of St Nicholas (13th-century) and St Peter (15th-century), the latter was restored after the 100 Years' War.

Coutances has a particularly pleasant terraced public garden, which once belonged to a private house. Clocks, cars and railway engines have been incorporated into the lavish flower beds. Views are extensive. In summer the garden and cathedral are floodlit and *son et lumière* performances held on certain days.

Coutances is the religious centre of the Cotentin department, of which it was once the capital, an honour now held by St Lô.

Dinner and overnight at La Moderne, Coutances.

Les Isles
Boulevard Maritime
50270 Barneville-Carteret
Tel: 33 04 90 76

Set right on the beach this hotel has a sheltered garden with tables and umbrellas from which to admire the white sweep of sand while sipping your aperitif.

Closed:	December and January
Rooms:	35
Credit cards:	All
Food:	Very reasonable fixed price menus. Lots of seafood.
Rating:	★★★

USEFUL INFORMATION: BARNEVILLE-CARTERET

Tourist Office:	Place Dr Auvret
	Tel: 33 04 90 58
Population:	2,327

USEFUL INFORMATION: CHERBOURG

Tourist Office:	2 Quai Alexandre III
	Tel: 33 43 52 02
Population:	89,855
Amenities:	Golf, port, aerodrome, parks

La Moderne
25 Boulevard Alsace-Lorraine
Coutances
Tel: 33 45 13 77

Closed:	15th December to 15th January
Rooms:	17
Facilities:	Parking, good value restaurant
Credit cards:	Eurocard, Visa
Rating:	★★★

For a rather splendid alternative take the D7/27 south-east out of Coutances for eight miles to:

Château de la Salle
50210 Montpichon (Cerisy)
Tel: 33 46 95 19

Set in a splendid 16th-century mansion built round a grand courtyard this hotel is a truly luxurious and elegant establishment. The decor and furnishings are sumptious and traditionally Norman in style. You can breakfast on a lovely, leafy terrace.

Closed:	2nd November to 20th March
Rooms:	10
Credit cards:	Carte Bleue, Visa, American Express, Diners
Food:	Very high standards. Le Délice du Bois Marquis, les Ris de Veau à l'Ancienne and La Feuillantine de Pommes au Caramel de Cidre are their specialities.
Rating:	★★★★★

USEFUL INFORMATION: COUTANCES

Population:	13,439
Amenities:	Cathedral, park

Criqueboeuf church, near Honfleur

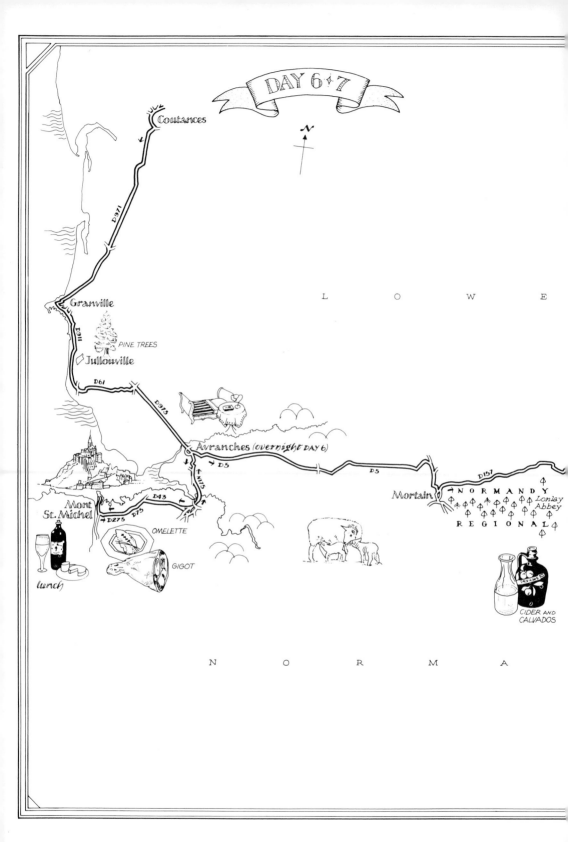

DAY 6 & 7

N

Coutances

D971

L O W E

Granville

D911

PINE TREES

Jullouville

D61

D973

Avranches (overnight day 6)

D5

D5

Mortain

D157

NORMANDY

Lonlay Abbey

REGIONAL

NID5

Mont St. Michel

D43

D275   D75

OMELETTE

GIGOT

lunch

CIDER AND CALVADOS

N   O   R   M   A

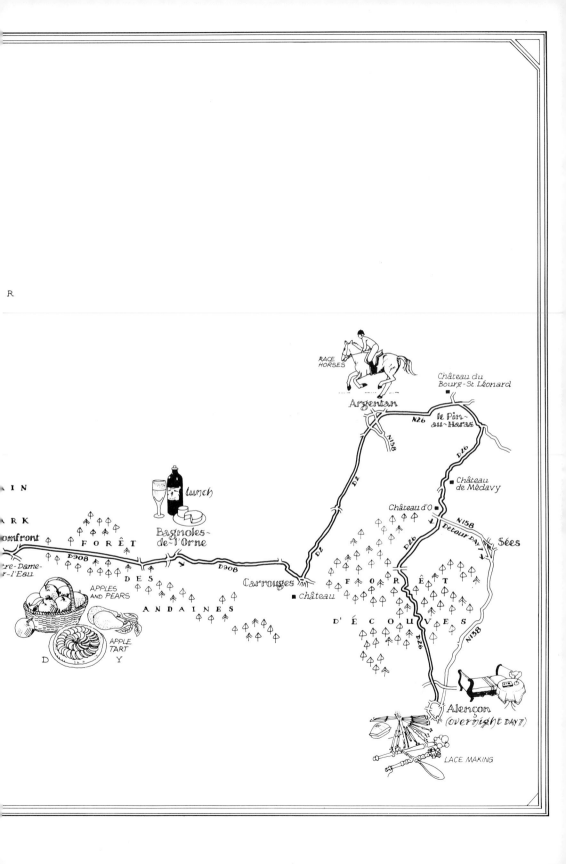

R

RACE
HORSES

Château du
Bourg - St Léonard

Argentan

N26

le Pin~
au~Haras

N158

D2

D26

Château
de Médavy

Château d'O

N158

lunch

Sées

Detour DAY 7

D26

Bagnoles~
de~l'Orne

A I N

R K

omfront

FORÊT

re-Dame-
r-l'Eau

D908

D908

Carrouges

château

FORÊT

D'ÉCOUVES

N158

APPLES
AND PEARS

DES

ANDAINES

D26

D

APPLE
TART

Y

Alençon

(overnight DAY 7)

LACE MAKING

Porte du Roi, Mont-St-Michel

DAY 6

Coutances to Avranches: approx. 64 miles.

From Coutances we continue south via the port of Granville to reach Mont-St-Michel ideally mid-morning. This must be for most the highlight of any holiday to Normandy, so allow plenty of time to examine this world-famous landmark. In the late afternoon we return to the mainland retracing the morning's route back to Avranches.

Breakfast at Coutances.

Leave Coutances by the D971 to Granville — a somewhat grim-looking old town surrounded by ramparts, and perched on a rocky spur. At the base lies an ordinary port but through the drawbridge you enter an almost unchanged 18th-century world behind the ramparts of the upper town. It should be of interest to the English as it was founded by them during the Hundred Years' War to consolidate their position on this part of the coast. The Germans who used it during the last war, turned it into a formidable stronghold. Granville boasts a casino, golf-course, aquarium, but not a very good beach. However, it is a favourite centre for yachtsmen. There are boat trips from here to Jersey and the Chausey Isles.

Further down the coast lies Jullouville, amid pine trees, beside an enormous stretch of sand — the sea here recedes for a mile.

I recommend travelling straight through Avranches (D61/973/175/43/275) to Mont-St-Michel for the mid-morning, giving you the best part of the day to visit this fairy-tale monument.

Mont-St-Michel

My first sight of Mont-St-Michel was early on a wet morning in 1966, its millenary year. This old walled abbey town built in tiers up a rock suddenly seemed to swing out upon the horizon, a blurred dreamlike image, a medieval mirage, suspended between earth and sky.

Its story is a fascinating mixture of history and geography. Centuries ago the whole of the bay in which it stands was a vast forest extending as far as the Channel Islands. The rocky summit on which St Michel now stands was first used by the Druids, then the Romans, then Christian hermits. After later tides had cut off the rock it was used as a place of refuge for people fleeing from the Vikings, and an oratory was built by St Aubert. Next came the pilgrims. In 966 Richard Duke of Normandy had the oratory replaced by a Bénédictine abbey (a picture of this can be seen in the Bayeux Tapestry). The abbey flourished, became a celebrated place of learning, but was burned down in 1203. The French king, Philippe-Auguste, in recompense, provided the means for the construction of La Merveille, the splendid edifice that stands there now.

It has had a turbulent history especially during the Hundred Years' War, but was gradually enlarged and became even grander and more beautiful. Its decline started during the reign of Louis XIV, when he appointed his favourites as Abbots. During the French Revolution, when the monks were made to leave, it was known as the Mount of Liberty. Napoleon had it used as a prison, which it remained until 1863. Restoration started in 1874, when it became a national monument. But it was not until 1966 that Bénédictine monks from St Wandrille returned to hold services in its great abbey church again.

Today, the old town and abbey of Mont-St-Michel is chiefly for pilgrims and tourists. The best time to come is on a weekday morning, preferably not in high season (July/August). Drive to Mont-St-Michel along a mile-long causeway across the sands. After parking, you can walk over a footbridge and through an entrance gate. Buildings climb the mount's steep rocky sides in terraces; the narrow street up to the abbey is lined with shops stacked with souvenirs. The name 'Merveille' refers only to the splendid Gothic abbey on the north side of the mount, a place fit for kings, as indeed many were entertained here. The cloisters, in particular, are very fine, and should not be missed.

It is a hard climb up but well worth it for the sight of the abbey and for the view which is to be had of the surrounding country from the terrace outside the church. On the river side is Normandy's boundary line, putting Mont-St-Michel just into the province. Beyond lies Brittany. In 1984 Mont-St-Michel was officially registered on the list of World Natural and Cultural Patrimony of UNESCO.

When visiting Mont-St-Michel, it is worth buying the more expensive *Visite Commentée* ticket, rather than just the admission one, as this will enable you to explore more of the abbey, such as the subterranean chapels and the steep *escalier de dentelle*. The garden is extra, but again worth it, this time for the good views of the abbey's architecture. Do not try and walk across the beach without a guide, as there are dangerous quicksands. Tides here race in like galloping horses, certainly faster than you are likely to be able to run.

Lunch at Mère Poulard, Mont-St-Michel.

Recrossing the causeway, retrace your steps to end the afternoon at Avranches.

Avranches

Avranches, situated so picturesquely on a hill above the Sées estuary, once possessed a cathedral, and was a Bishop's see from 511 to 1790. The cathedral was demolished in 1794, during the French Revolution. You can still see the paving stone — known locally as 'the Platform' — on which Henry II knelt to do penance for the murder of Thomas-à-Becket, on the site of the former cathedral.

The museum inside the Bishop's Lodgings, beside the old Bishop's Palace, houses a unique collection of manuscripts from Mont-St-Michel. You shouldn't miss seeing some of the remarkable illustrated texts.

Avranches has two distinctions. One is that it was from here that General Patton launched his famous assault, smashing the German counter-attack from Mortain, which then carried his 3rd army through Brittany and Le Mans in August, 1944. To commemorate this event a monument is sited in a square on soil and by trees especially flown here from America. Thus it may be said to stand on American soil. The other is that it was the see of St Aubert, founder of Mont-St-Michel. His skull in the church of St Gervase and St Protase shows the dent supposedly made by the imperious archangel Michael, when his instructions to build an oratory on the rock were at first disregarded by St Aubert.

Avranches, like Coutances with whom there is no little rivalry, also boasts a fine botanical garden. However, it is not such a good one. It possesses no tree for instance that grows two different types of leaves! However, from its terrace is one of the best views in France, especially if seen by moonlight, that of the rocky island, town and abbey of Mont-St-Michel.

Dinner and overnight at Auberge St Michel, Avranches.

Hôtel Restaurant La Mère Poulard
50115 Le Mont St Michel
Tel: 33 60 14 01

Although is has been thoroughly smartened up and modernised they do cook the famous omelette at the same fire that Annette Poulard used at the turn of the century.

Open:	All year
Rooms:	22
Facilities:	Piano bar, billiards and bridge rooms.
Credit cards:	All
Food:	Rather smart, try Salade de foie de Canarde frais et sa pôelée de pétoncles
Rating:	★★★★

USEFUL INFORMATION: MONT-ST-MICHEL

Tourist Office:	Corps de Garde des Bourgeois (March-Oct.) Tel: 33 60 14 30
Population:	80
Amenities:	As the island is completely surrounded by water at high tide it would be wise to check the tide times before venturing across the sands.

If Mont-St-Michel seems too crowded drive a couple of miles down the road to Beauvoir where there is a charmingly renovated hotel whose restaurant specialises in local dishes.

Hôtel le Beauvoir
51070 Beauvoir
Tel: 33 60 09 39

Hôtel le Beauvoir (cont'd.)

Closed:	November. Restaurant closed on Tuesdays.
Rooms:	19
Credit cards:	Carte Bleu
Food:	A varied good quality menu.
Rating:	★★★

Auberge St Michel
7 Place Général Patton
Avranches
Tel: 33 58 01 91

A pretty, creeper-covered, old Norman building. Tables under umbrellas overlook a pleasant tree-lined open space with a memorial to General Patton in the centre. Very close to all the town's interesting churches and museums. The dining room has real fires in the stone fireplace.

Closed:	16th November to 1st May and Sunday evenings and Mondays.
Rooms:	22
Facilities:	Restaurant, Parking
Credit cards:	Visa, Eurocard
Food:	Good value
Rating:	★★

Le Croix d'Or
83 Rue Constitution
Avranches
Tel: 33 58 04 88

Closed:	Mid November to mid March
Rooms:	30
Facilities:	Restaurant, garden, parking
Credit cards:	Visa
Rating:	★★★

USEFUL INFORMATION: AVRANCHES

Tourist Office:	Rue Général de Gaulle
	Tel: 33 58 00 22
Population:	10,419
Amenities:	Wonderful view of Mont-St-Michel from Botanic gardens planted by the Franciscans.

Mont-St-Michel

DAY 7

Avranches to Alençon: approx. 120 miles.

Leaving Avranches the route crosses the south-western edge of Normandy into the department of Orne, reputed above all for horse-breeding and its châteaux. We cross the Normandie-Maine regional park first to Domfront then to lunch at the wooded resort of Bagnoles-de-l'Orne. After visiting Carrouges Château, the route turns north to Argentan where horses are the chief concern and livelihood of many. The lordly setting and style of Le Pin Stud reflects the high regard in which horse-breeding is held in France. Then the route winds its way past the lush green forest of Écouves to Alençon.

Breakfast at Avranches.

Leave Avranches on the D5 to take the most scenic route across the south-western stretch of Normandy. From Mortain to Domfront (D157/22) the road, at times fairly steep, takes you through the northern edge of the Normandie-Maine regional park.

Off the D22 before Domfront lies Lonlay Abbey — a Romanesque transept and Gothic chancel are the visible remains of what was once a massive early Romanesque church. But as you wander around the vast transept you can easily envision the scale of the original building.

As you enter Domfront visit the rather lovely Notre-Dame-sur-l'Eau (12th-century). Here the grandmother of St Louis — Louis IX (1214–70) France's most saintly king — was baptised in 1162 and, four years' later, Thomas-à-Becket celebrated the Christmas mass in this church.

Domfront, whose name comes from St Front or Frontius, stands along a rocky crest above the Varenne. It was once a small straggling border town, strategically important and belonging to the notorious Bellême family. Today's town is set amid a landscape of apple orchards; its pedestrianised cobbled street is usually thronged with tourists.

Driving on through the scenic Forêt des Andaines (D908) one comes upon Bagnoles-de-l'Orne, one of my favourite Norman towns. A spa resort — its waters are to be bathed in, not tasted — it is pictorially sited beside a lake, surrounded by forests. Bagnoles is a relaxing place in which to spend a few days holiday, also a good centre for further explorations, especially into Swiss Normandy (see Day 3).

Lunch at Le Café de Paris, Bagnoles-de-l'Orne.

The department of Orne, you will notice, is a hilly and pastoral countryside, best known for its cattle and dairy products — it is the birthplace of Camembert cheese, also a famous and powerful breed of draught horses, the Normandy percheron. On one side lie the rich undulating plains of Alençon and Argentan while the western part merges with the Amorican massif and wooded bocage.

Carrouges

Carrouges château (D908), fortified in the 12th century by the Counts of Carrouges, later passed into the hands of the Tillières family, who retained it until 1936. This impressive ornate redbrick and granite residence is surrounded by a moat. Its special attractions are its elegant gatehouse — note the wrought-iron gates — the state rooms on the first floor (fine Renaissance and classical-style decorations and rich furnishings), the monumental staircase of honour and portrait gallery.

Argentan

Argentan (D2 northwards then D924) was so badly damaged in the last war — the final battle of Normandy the battle of the Falaise–Mortain pocket was fought near here — that it had to be completely rebuilt and there is little of the old-style town to see. It was best known for its 15th- to 17th-century church, St Germain, and the Renaissance St Martin — now both restored — and lace-making. Nuns run a lace workshop in the Bénédictine Abbey (2 Rue de l'Abbaye) and in the museum of stitch lace you can see the Point d'Argentan stitch, created here, and to which the nuns have exclusive rights.

However, Argentan's major attraction is the Hippodrome where on two mornings a week you can see the famous horses put through their paces. For, not only are the celebrated percheron horses bred in this region but at Le Pin-au-Haras, (N26 from Argentan) is Le Pin Stud — the Horses' Versailles. The building (1716–1728) was designed by Jules Hardouin-Mansart, the architect responsible for Louis XIV's great folly, as a nursery for army horses. The main courtyard is horseshoe-shaped; the wide avenues open on to perspectives of the mansion. Note the spacious brick and stone stables. Now a stud farm, it houses about 200 stallions, many with famous names in the horse-breeding world. Entrance is free, a groom will show you around the stables and you can see the horses setting off and returning from their daily exercises.

Detour

Off the N26, before Le Pin Stud, stands the Château du Bourg-St-Léonard, a monument to the *Ancien Régime*. It was built just before the French Revolution and was obviously designed with such sumptuous entertainments as theatricals and balls in mind. Much of its decor — panelling, tapestries and furnishings — are original and date from the Louis XV period.

You will pass the Château de Médavy on the way from Le-Pin-au-Haras to Château d'O (D26). Although not open to visitors (except the stud farm by appointment) the exterior is worth viewing. Moats fed by the Orne, two 15th-century towers, crowned by lantern domes standing before the somewhat severe early 18th-century château, remind one that it was once a stronghold.

Château d'O

Judging by appearances, Château d'O has come straight out of a fairytale. Built out of rose-coloured bricks, it is an attractive mix of sloping roofs, steeples, turrets and gables, somehow blending the Gothic and Renaissance styles. All this is reflected in the broad moat, spanned by a narrow bridge. An extensive surrounding park and woods complete the ensemble. You may picnic beside the lake, watched by graceful swans, or eat in the 12th-century Commandery, now the Ferme d'O Restaurant, which serves regional specialities.

Detour II

From Château d'O take the N158 to Sées. There is not much to see at Sées, a sleepy if once important ecclesiastical town, apart from its lofty Gothic cathedral (note the 13th-century stained glass and rose windows and the rather sweet 14th-century Virgin and Child statue). There is a museum of religious art open at Sées during the season. Continue to Alençon on the N138.

Drive south (D26) through the Écouves forest, one of the loveliest stretches of woodland in France, to Alençon. The Perseigne forest (lying either side of the main road) is also handsome with many paths to explore and picnic areas.

Alençon

Alençon, a central position on many roads, and a key town in the Mortain–Falaise pocket was the first town to be liberated by French General Le Clerc in World War Two. It was the birthplace of Ste Thérèse, second patroness of France, and a great favourite with the armed forces. It is also the home of hand-made lace, an art which alas is fast dying out. You can visit the school of lace in Rue du Pont-Neuf — its small museum contains Point d'Alençon worn by Marie Antionette (some of the lace is so delicate it has to be looked at under a magnifying glass). Alençon was fortunate in that it escaped much war damage and has retained her old monuments — the castle of the powerful Duke of Alençon (now a prison), church of Notre-Dame, a beautiful 14th- to 15th-century structure, but the tower, transept and chancel are of the 18th century, also the picturesque medieval streets and houses in the St Léonard quarter where, from a central crossroads, evocatively-named roads offer a variety of choices.

To the south lie the Alpes Mancelles, not exactly alpine (highest point is only 1200 ft) but an interesting and pleasant landscape with many swift-flowing streams, gorges and heather-clad hills.

Dinner and overnight at Le Chapeau Rouge, Alençon.

Hôtel Bois Joli
Avenue Phillippe-du-Rosier
61140 Bagnoles-de-l'Orne
Tel: 33 37 92 77

Looking rather Tyrolean in a wooded setting this hotel offers reasonably priced food, including a Soufflé glace à la Bagnolese — a suitably frivolous dish for this holiday town.

Closed:	December to March
Rooms:	20
Credit cards:	American Express, Visa, Eurocard
Food:	The specialities include Ecrevisses à la Bordelaise and Gratin de Langouste.
Rating:	★★★

USEFUL INFORMATION: BAGNOLES-DE-L'ORNE

Tourist Office:	Place Gare (March-Sept.)
	Tel: 33 37 85 66
Population:	783
Amenities:	Golf, casino, lake, park

Hôtel Restaurant Le Chapeau Rouge
1 Boulevard Duchamp
or 117 Rue de Bretagne
61000 Alençon
Tel: (Hotel) 33 26 20 23
    (Restaurant) 33 26 23 75

This hotel is near the centre of town and is run by an Englishman, Mr Bets, who is also the chef.

Open:	All year.
Rooms:	16
Credit cards:	Carte Bleu, Mastercard, Eurocard
Food:	Varied reasonable menu, try Garibas (large shrimps) in a whisky sauce.
Rating:	★★

Grand Cerf
21 rue St-Blaise
61000 Alençon
Tel: 33 26 00 51

Closed:	29 July to 14 October, and 15 December to 15 January, and Sundays.
Rooms:	33
Credit cards:	Visa, American Express, Eurocard
Rating:	★★★

USEFUL INFORMATION: ARGENTAN

Tourist Office:	Avenue Pasteur (15 June-15 Sept.)
Population:	3,424

USEFUL INFORMATION: ALENÇON

Tourist Office:	Maison d'Ozé
Population:	32,526

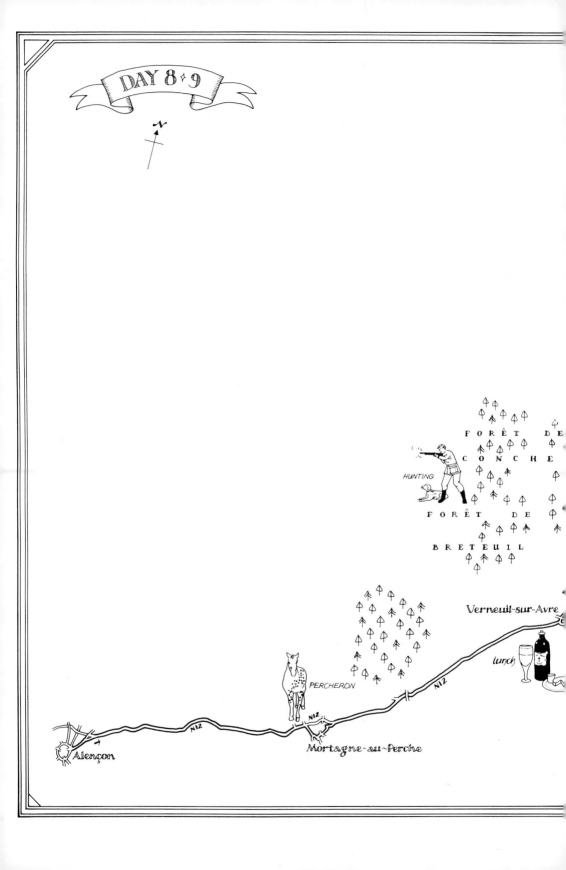

DAY 8 ♦ 9

N

FORÊT DE
CONCHE

HUNTING

FORÊT DE

BRETEUIL

Verneuil-sur-Avre

lunch

N12

PERCHERON

N12

N12

Alençon

N12

Mortagne-au-Perche

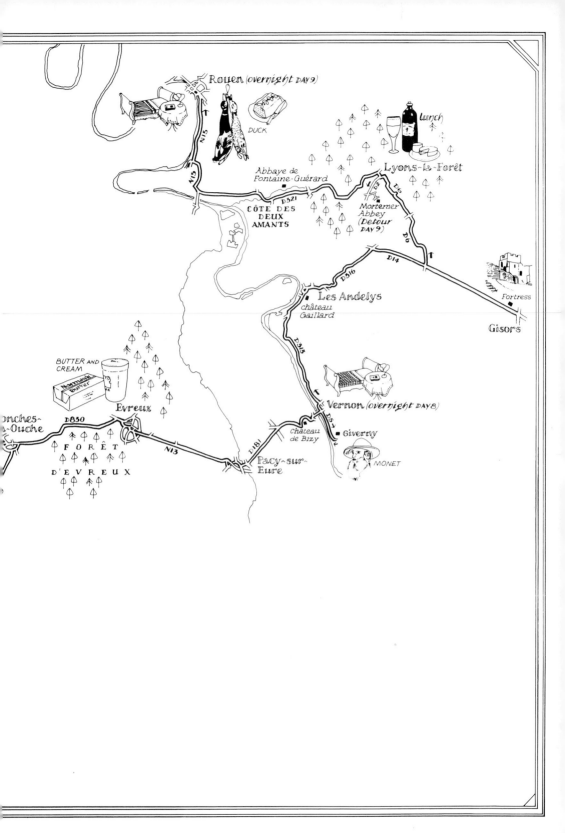

Rouen (overnight DAY 9)

DUCK

lunch

Lyons-la-Forêt

N 15

N 15

Abbaye de
Fontaine-Guérard

D 321

CÔTE DES
DEUX
AMANTS

Mortemer
Abbey
(Detour
DAY 9)

D 12

D 715

D 6

D 14

D 316

Fortress

Les Andelys

château
Gaillard

D 313

Gisors

BUTTER AND
CREAM

Normandy
Butter

Evreux

Vernon (overnight DAY 8)

D 181

D 5

château
de Bizy

Giverny

MONET

onches-
-Ouche

D 830

FORÊT

N 13

Pacy-sur-
Eure

D'EVREUX

DAY 8

Alençon to Vernon: approx. 94 miles.

Leaving Alençon we cross the southern stretch of the department of Eure through wooded hunting territories to Verneuil for lunch and on to visit Évreux (the capital of Eure) and the Château de Bizy in the afternoon. It is well worth making a detour to the riverside village of Giverny, where painter Claude Monet lived from 1883 to his death in 1926. His home, very well restored and now a museum, shows reproductions of his work, while the garden, his inspiration, has been replanted according to his original design. Overnight at Vernon.

Breakfast at Alençon.

As the route (N12) approaches Mortagne-au-Perche, so the surrounding terrain becomes hillier. This is the homeland of the Normandy Percheron, a dray horse well-known for its pulling power and great strength. You will probably see some of these dapple grey or black good-natured beasts grazing in the fields. From Mortagne, standing on a hill, are splendid views over the undulating countryside, especially from its public gardens. Although old — note the distinctive brown-tiled rooftops — Mortagne has expanded considerably from the small capital of the Perche region it once was. But it is still traditional and conservative as you will see if you sit in a café in the central square and watch the world go by. Its colourful Saturday market is worth a visit. If here in March look out for the Black Pudding Fair.

The road north-eastwards to Verneuil passes through forests stocked with game and small lakes.

Verneuil-sur-Avre

Verneuil, along with Tillières and Nonancourt, once formed the Avre defence line on the Norman French border. It is a distinguished-looking little town, descended from the fortified city created in the 12th century by Henry I, when Duke of Normandy. Its best known features are Ste Magdalene church, especially its tower (end of 15th-century, beginning of 16th-century), 150 ft high, built in three stages, richly-decorated, and crowned by an octagonal lantern; and Notre-Dame church, built in red stone (12th-century and contains many early 16th-century statues of saints, mostly carved by local sculptors), which lies in a tangle of old streets. Stout circular Tour Grise was built by Henry I as part of the town's fortifications.

The Department of Eure, lying astride the Lower Seine, south of Seine Maritime is a leafy region of many rivers. Trees border the water, shade the valleys and climb the hillsides. Towns are small, most people here live in villages. Tall manor houses are surrounded by farms. The region is spread across a large area. If you have extra time to spend in this department then châteaux to see and/or visit are Beaumesnil (17th-century, majestic brick and stone, Louis XIII style), La Mesangère (17th-century, park designed by Le Nôtre) and Acquigny (16th-century). Of the many abbeys and castles once scattered over the countryside, only ruins are to be seen. Bec-Hellouin abbey north of Brionne, (mostly 17th- and 18th-century) cradle of Anglo-Norman culture and religious development, and where intellectual and religious life still continue, is an exception.

Lunch at the Hostellerie du Clos, Verneuil.

Heading northwards past the Fôret de Conches, the D840 leads to Conches-en-Ouche. Conches, set on a spur above a bend in the Rouloir river, was fortunate in that it was little damaged by the war: also a ring road diverts away heavy traffic. Thus it has retained some of its picturesque medieval character and atmosphere as represented by narrow streets and dark-timbered buildings. Surrounded by forests it has become a major hunting centre. This is reflected in the restaurants where delectable game terrines are served. To see is Ste Foy church (note Renaissance stained-glass windows); also a ruined keep, surrounded by 12th-century towers in the Town Hall gardens.

The D830 continues to Évreux, capital of Eure.

Évreux

Évreux, despite a history of fire and destruction, exudes a pleasant air of cheerful busyness. Built around the numerous branches of the Iton river and with many stone bridges to cross, it could be described as a watery town. After the destruction of the last war — its centre burned for almost a week — the town was rebuilt in such a way as to combine old and new to picturesque effect. There is a pretty walk around the old ramparts. The cathedral and Bishop's Palace, enclosed within the walls, are covered in greenery which reflects in the weedy, moated water below.

Because of the town's stormy history, the cathedral has been repeatedly destroyed and rebuilt over a number of centuries and so styles date from the 11th to 18th century. Noteworthy, are its richly decorated north and west facades and 15th- and 16th-century windows around the choir. The museum in the Bishop's Palace houses a good collection of Gallo–Roman and medieval remains. St Taurin, the old Bénédictine abbey church, possesses a silver gilt and enamel reliquary of its saint.

Next to the public gardens stands the Capuchin Friars' Monastery. Some of the building dates back to the 17th century. The cloisters are particularly fine (note the moral maxims engraved on the panels) and can be visited whenever the school, which uses this part of the building, is closed i.e. Thursdays, Sundays and during the Summer vacation.

Continue on the N13/D181 to Vernon on the Seine.

Château de Bizy

On the outskirts of Vernon stands the imposing Château de Bizy in its park and at the end of long tree-lined avenues. A semi-circular courtyard, statues and fountains enhance its calm classical style. Bizy was built in 1741. It was once renowned for its stables, inspired by those of Versailles, but which now hold vintage cars. It has had a number of owners. Commissioned by Field-Marshal Fouquet, it later belonged to King Louis XV, the Duke of Penthièvre and to King Louis-Philippe. Baron Schickler was responsible for the present-day Italian-style palace castle. Inside are 18th-century tapestries, Empire-style furniture and an exhibition of Napoleonic souvenirs.

Vernon

Vernon, once a gateway to Normandy, and therefore a fortress town, has had quite an exciting history. Today it is merely a very pleasant, leafy riverside resort, with not very much old left to see.

Detour

South on the D5 from Vernon lies Giverny, where Claude Monet lived from 1883 to 1926. Massive restoration work has been done on the property so that the house, gardens, studio, even the Water Garden have been brought back to the condition in which Monet left them. The gardens have been replanted as they once were, and inside the house his collection of Japanese engravings has been arranged as Monet placed them over fifty years ago. The enormous attention to detail is most impressive and I highly recommend a visit.

Dinner and overnight at Hôtel Évreux, Vernon.

Hostellerie du Clos
98 Rue da le Ferte Vidame
27130 Verneuil-sur-Avre
Tel: 32 32 21 81

Another splendid Relais and Châteaux. An elaborately brick-patterned house, set in lush gardens with a lovely dining terrace. The fixed price menus are very reasonable considering the high standard of cuisine and the luxuriant surroundings.

Closed:	November to Easter. Restaurant closed Mondays.
Rooms:	9
Facilities:	Bar, restaurant, gardens.
Credit cards:	Visa, Mastercard, American Express, Diners Club.
Food:	Rather grand, very much dependent on the day's marketing.
Rating:	★★★★★

For a considerably more modest alternative:

Le Grand Sultan
30 Rue Poissonerie
27130 Verneuil-sur-Avre
Tel: 32 32 13 41

USEFUL INFORMATION: VERNEUIL-SUR-AVRE

Tourist Office:	129 Place Madeleine
	Tel: 32 32 17 17
Population:	6,926

Hôtel Évreux (le Relais Normande)
7 Place d'Évreux
27200 Vernon
Tel: 32 21 16 12

Open:	All year, restaurant closed on Sundays.
Rooms:	20
Facilities:	Bar, restaurant
Credit cards:	Carte Bleu, Eurocard, Diners Club, American Express
Food:	Reasonably priced
Rating:	★★★

Another hotel practically opposite is:

Hôtel Strasbourg
6 Place Évreux
27200 Vernon
Tel: 32 51 23 12

Open:	All year, restaurant closed Sunday and Monday in Winter.
Rooms:	23
Facilities:	Bar, restaurant
Credit cards:	Carte Bleu, Eurocard
Food:	Good value, try Canard à la Rouennaise
Rating:	★★

USEFUL INFORMATION: VERNON

Tourist Office:	Passage Pasteur
	Tel: 32 51 39 60
Population:	23,464
Amenities:	Claude Monet Museum, Giverny

DAY 9

Vernon to Rouen: approx. 71 miles.

From Vernon it is a short trip up the Seine valley to the hauntingly beautiful
Les Andelys. Turning north from the Seine via the old fortress of Gisors, we
stop for lunch in Lyons-la-Forêt. The afternoon is spent in Rouen.

Old shop in Rouen

Breakfast at Vernon.

Cross the Seine and travel north along the D313, for a picturesque drive bordered by the river on one side and forests on the other.

Les Andelys

Arriving at Les Andelys, you will immediately see why the twin villages Petit and Grand are celebrated chiefly for Château Gaillard, which rises white and gaunt above the town, almost as if it had grown out of the chalky soil. A car can be driven most of the way to it, but the last bit has to be done on foot. Château Gaillard is now merely a ruin, a shell, but nevertheless it is still one of the most attractive and romantic-looking castles in the whole of Normandy. The view from the top is spectacular — perhaps one of the most impressive in the Seine valley.

Gaillard was built by Richard the Lionheart, incorporating everything known to 12th-century military architects, and was intended to bar the French king's way into Normandy via the Seine river. Alas, it was taken by Philippe-Auguste in 1204. During the Hundred Years' War it changed hands many times. France's Henry IV beseiged it for two years during the Wars of Religion and, when it finally fell, he had it dismantled. Some of its stones were used in the construction of other buildings, such as the convent of the Capuchins at Andelys. From its site, there is a magnificent and grandiose view over the Seine.

Les Andelys was the home of Nicholas Poussin (whose *Coriolan* is on view in the city museum) and of Blanchard the great balloonist.

Gisors

Gisors, further on along the D316/14, was long contested by the English and French. Its stern, 11th- to 12th-century ruined fortress still dominates the old frontier town, so picturesquely divided by the Epte river. To visit are the fortress garden and 12th- to 16th-century St Gervais-en-St Protais, a mixture of styles (the monumental west front is Renaissance) but the effect is harmonious. If you pass through on a Saturday you will find a lively market in full swing.

Normandy is a region of superb forests, especially in the south. Although alas like southern England, the province suffered badly in the October gale of 1987, losing perhaps 20% of its trees, fortunately this was mainly in the Manche area and along the coast.

Lyons-la-Forêt

You can drive from Gisors to Lyons-la-Forêt (D14/6) whose surrounding forest was once the favourite hunting grounds of the Dukes of Normandy. Beech and oak trees grow to an enormous size in the chalky soil and tree experts from far and wide come to study its silviculture. Nearby is the ruined 12th-century Bénédictine (later Cistercian) abbey at Mortemer (D2/151), one of Christendom's most beautiful medieval relics, standing amid trees beside a spring.

Lyons-la-Forêt with many good hotels and restaurants and a fine centre for further explorations, is a delightful picture-book small town. Half-timbered, colour-washed houses centring on the old 18th-century timber-roofed market hall make it most appropriately a town of the trees, a truly sylvan place. Its 15th-century church, with timber belfry, contains many wooden statues.

Lunch at La Licorne, Lyons-la-Forêt.

West through the forest (D321) lies the ruined Abbaye de Fontaine-Guérard. As you approach the Seine on your left note the high escarpment — the Côte des Deux Amants. Legend states that the two lovers in question were Raoul, a handsome peasant, and Caliste, daughter of the Baron of St Pierre. To prove his worthiness the Baron demanded that Raoul run, without stopping, to the top of the escarpment carrying Caliste in his arms. Raoul did it but collapsed and died of exhaustion at the top. Caliste died at his side.

Rouen

And so to Rouen (N15), old but exhuberant and a haven for gourmets. Rouen, the Ville Musée and capital of Upper Normandy, was also badly damaged during the last war. Fortunately, though, the robust timber frames of the medieval houses withstood the bomb blasts and have been reconstructed so that the character of the old streets still remains.

Called Rotomagus by the Romans, Rouen first evolved on the river banks where a bridge could be built at the start of the bend, protected by high cliffs. There are therefore some good viewpoints of the town and port from Rouen corniche, Ste Catherine's Hill and Bonsecours.

After Rollo had agreed the St Clair-sur-Epte pact, he became a Christian and was baptised at Rouen, capital of his new duchy. Rouen had a hard time during the Hundred Years' War. The Renaissance was its golden era when many fine stone mansions were built and existing houses ornamented. Her traders took their goods — chiefly linen, silk and rich cloth — all over the world. Predominantly Protestant, she suffered hardship during the Wars of Religion and especially after the Revocation of the Edict of Nantes in 1685, when a large number of the population, mostly engaged in the textile industry, emigrated. The development of the port in the 20th century led to considerable industrial expansion, and the damage caused by the last war enabled a better-planned city to be built. Most modern construction is confined to the left bank of the Seine so that the old quarter on the right is not spoiled by discordant post-war architecture.

Narrow streets mean that old Rouen — 'a labyrinth of delight' (Ruskin) — is best explored on foot. Start from Place du Vieux Marché, the old market square although now much enlarged, where Jeanne d'Arc was burned at the stake on 30th May, 1431.

The square, now surrounded by restaurants, cafés and old houses (one contains the Joan of Arc Museum), has been reconstructed, and possesses a neo-medieval market hall and Ste Jeanne d'Arc church (superb 16th-century stained glass windows). Her statue is set against the church and looks in the direction of the stake, where now stands a 60 ft cross. The Rue du Gros-Horloge is dominated by a magnificent 14th-century clock, very colourful in red, blue and gold, set above a 16th-century arch. This is the city's best known landmark. The road leads under the arch to Place de la Cathédrale.

Notre-Dame cathedral, restored after the considerable damage it received, has a front facade which bristles with intricate carvings. It is considered to be the finest Gothic cathedral in France, while the 19th-century open-work iron spire — 425 ft tall — is the highest. The cathedral's main features are the two towers and spire, all quite different, yet seeming to harmonise. It was constructed chiefly during the 13th century, after a devastating fire. Parts of it were added later in the 15th and 16th centuries. To note inside (surprisingly

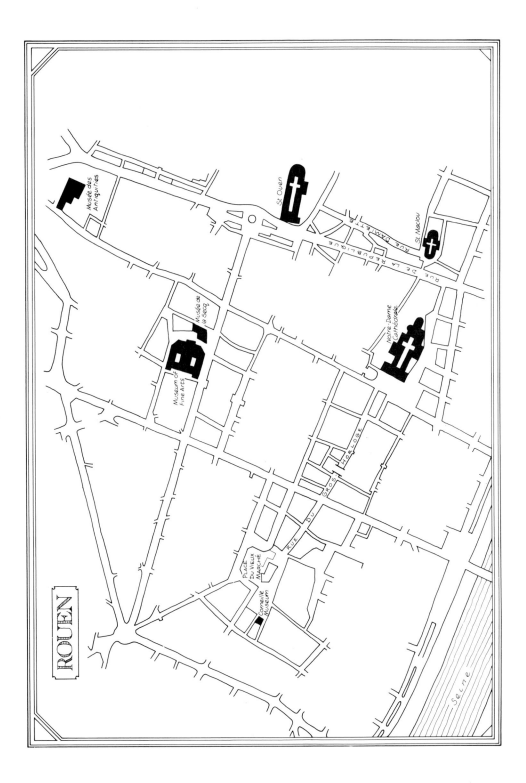

ROUEN

Musée des Antiquités

St Ouen

St Maclou

RUE DE LA RÉPUBLIQUE

RUE DAMIETTE

RUE ST VIVIEN

Musée de la Secq

Museum of Fine Arts

Notre-Dame Cathédrale

RUE DU GROS HORLOGE

RUE DU

PLACE DU VIEUX MARCHÉ

Corneille Museum

Seine

austere in comparison to the outside) are the lantern tower, at the cross of the transept, the 13th- and 14th-century stained-glass windows, a delicate staircase leading to the libraries, and the tombs of early dukes and 16th-century Cardinals of Amboise (Renaissance patrons of the arts).

St Maclou is behind the cathedral — across Rue de la République — and is a masterpiece of Flamboyant-Gothic (built 1437–1517). It has a magnificent five-gabled portal and carved wooden door. After exploring the lane and its cloister, return to the front and take old Rue Damiette on the right, and continue via Rue des Boucheries St Ouen to St Ouen, an excellent example of later Gothic (1318–1519). Its west face, replaced between 1845 and 1851, presents a somewhat cold and unimaginative facade, but St Ouen is particularly noted for its beautiful interior — the purity of the nave, its chancel and organ and the magnificent rose windows.

Rouen has some good museums. There is the Museum of Fine Arts (Rouen pottery and a very fine collection of paintings, including Impressionists), and the Musée de la Secq (specialising in wrought-iron). The Musée des Antiquités has a fascinating regional collection of relics from Gallo-Roman, Merovingian and Renaissance times. There is a museum in the house of the classical dramatist Corneille (1606–1684) and a museum of medieval history in the hospital where the surgeon father of novelist Gustave Flaubert (1821–80) practised his skills, also a museum in the house at Croisset where Flaubert wrote his celebrated *Madame Bovary*.

Because Rouen is such an attractive old Norman town, it may cause you severe problems unless you have already booked up at a hotel. Accommodation is difficult to find, and especially so, in the summer. There are a number of reasonably-priced restaurants in and around Place du Vieux Marché.

Dinner and overnight at Rouen.

Hôtel de la Licorne
27480 Lyons-la-Forêt
Tel: 32 49 62 02

A thatched house surrounded by trees. Real fires and lots of wood and beams inside.

Closed:	16 December to 21 February, restaurant closed Sundays and Mondays in Winter.
Rooms:	22
Facilities:	Bar, restaurant, garden.
Credit cards:	Visa, Carte Bleu, American Express, Eurocard, Diners Club
Food:	Varied, interesting menu
Rating:	★★★★

USEFUL INFORMATION: LYONS-LA-FORÊT

Tourist Office:	à la Mairie
	Tel: 32 49 60 87
Population:	734

Hôtel de la Cathédrale
12 Rue St Romain
76000 Rouen
Tel: 35 71 57 95

A lovely old building with a stunning view of the Cathedral at the end of the narrow street. This hotel does not have its own restaurant, but it is charming as well as central. There are suggestions for eating overleaf.

Open:	All year.
Rooms:	24
Credit cards:	Carte Bleu, Visa, Mastercard
Rating:	★★★

If you prefer a restaurant in the hotel:

Hôtel de Dieppe
Place Bernard-Tissot
76000 Rouen
Tel: 35 71 96 00

Opposite the station and near the old part of town (5 minutes' walk), this is much more of a large town establishment.

Open:	All year.
Rooms:	42
Facilities:	Colour TV
Credit cards:	Carte Bleu, Visa, American Express, Diners Club
Food:	Smart, for example, Canéton Rouennais à la presse (prepared in the dining room before the customer).
Rating:	★★★★

USEFUL INFORMATION: ROUEN

Tourist Office:	25 Place Cathédrale
	Tel: 35 71 41 77
Population:	105,083
Amenities:	Cathedral, the old town, museums, golf

Suggested restaurants:

La Pascaline
5 Rue Poterne
76000 Rouen
Tel: 35 89 67 44

A jolly brasserie.

Open:	All year.
Credit cards:	Carte Bleu
Food:	Varied and very reasonable. Comptoir de Salade and Pied de Mouton Rouennais are considered their specialities.
Rating:	★★

Le Bois Chenu
23/5 Place de la Pucelle d'Orléans
76000 Rouen
Tel: 35 71 19 54

A lovely timbered building in the heart of the old town.

Open:	All year.
Credit cards:	Diners Club, American Express, Mastercard
Food:	Varied, reasonably priced menu.
Rating:	★★

Chez Dufour
67 bis Rue St Nicholas
76000 Rouen
Tel: 35 71 90 62

Another beautiful old building combined with good food, particularly oysters.

Closed:	Sunday evenings and Mondays
Credit cards:	Carte Bleu, Visa
Food:	Lots of fish
Rating:	★★★★

La Couronne
31 Place Vieux-Marché
76000 Rouen
Tel: 35 71 40 90

A genuine fourteenth-century Norman building.

Closed:	Sunday evenings
Credit cards:	American Express, Visa, Eurocard
Rating:	★★★★

Maison Gill
60 Rue St Nicholas
76000 Rouen
Tel: 35 71 16 14

Closed:	22nd August to 15th September, 1st to 19th February and Monday lunch and Sundays
Credit cards:	American Express, Visa, Eurocard
Food:	Minestrone de crustacés, a winter speciality
Rating:	★★★★

And just outside Rouen:

Le Vieux Moulin
3 Rue Samuel-Lecoeur
76820 Bapeaume-les-Rouen
Tel: 35 36 39 59

The restaurant is set in a wonderful thirteenth-century building, full of beams.

Open:	All year
Credit cards:	Diners Club, American Express
Food:	Live lobsters and langoustes
Rating:	★★★

St-Ouen, Rouen

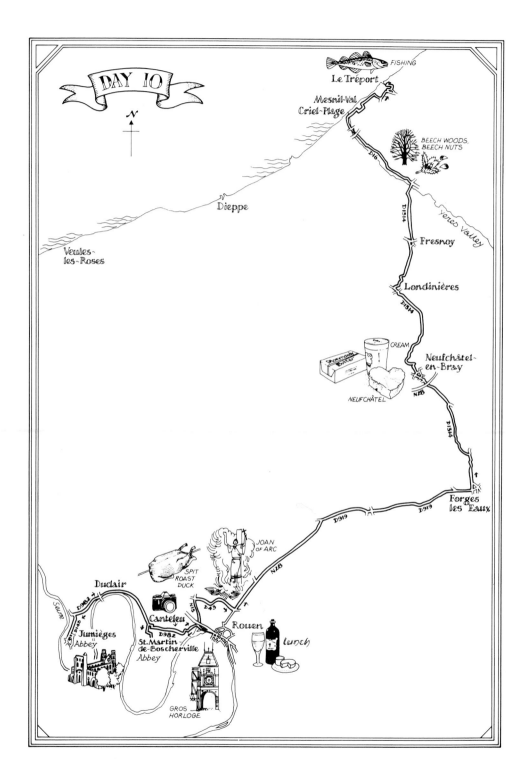

DAY 10

N

FISHING

Le Tréport

Mesnil-Val
Criel-Plage

BEECH WOODS,
BEECH NUTS

Dieppe

Veules-
les-Roses

Fresnoy

Londinières

CREAM

Neufchâtel-
en-Bray

NEUFCHÂTEL

Forges
les Eaux

D919

D919

JOAN
OF ARC

SPIT
ROAST
DUCK

Duclair

Canteleu

Rouen

lunch

Jumièges
Abbey

St.Martin
de-Boscherville
Abbey

GROS
HORLOGE

DAY 10

Rouen to Le Tréport: approx. 100 miles.

As there is so much to see in Rouen, you may well wish to remain in the town for the morning. However, I highly recommend a short trip westward, down the Seine valley to Jumièges Abbey. The ruins at Jumièges are one of France's most famous landmarks. In the afternoon we set off northwards, via the spa town of Forges-les-Eaux, for Le Tréport, a seaside resort just north of Dieppe.

Breakfast at Rouen.

Because Rouen is such an interesting old town you will probably wish to continue your explorations during the morning and maybe refresh yourself at one of the many deliciously inviting patisseries. But if you have time I would recommend a short morning trip westwards from Rouen to Jumièges.

Jumièges Abbey.

The D982/143 leads to Jumièges Abbey, so splendidly set beside the Seine, and one of France's largest and most beautiful ruins. This important centre of western learning survived pillaging and war, also suppression during the French Revolution. Then alas, although its precious library was saved, the building was sold to a merchant from Canteleu, who began using it as a stone quarry. Eventually in 1852 a new owner set about preserving what remained. Since 1947 it has belonged to the nation.

The mellow grey ruins which have often been compared to Fountains Abbey and Rievalaux in Yorkshire are most impressive, certainly photogenic. A roofless nave, overlooked by a wide gallery, is some 89 feet high, while twin octagonal towers rise 141 feet either side of the main door. Make time to visit St Pierre church (Norman Carolingian and 13th- and 14th-century), the chapterhouse (early 12th-century), cloister and store room which form part of the complex.

Return (D143/982) via the riverside resort Duclair, somewhat heavy in style, but agreeable enough. Duck is a local gastronomic speciality. Tuesday is market day here.

St Martin-de-Boscherville is the third great abbey of the Lower Seine and its church, St George (11th- to 12th-century) is still in use. It was saved from desecration because it became the parish church at the time of the Revolution. The building has a unity of style and proportion. The facade is plain but the main door is decorated with typical Norman Romanesque motifs: the capitals are remarkably delicate.

Chalky cliffs and wooded hills follow: the road winds away from the river through pretty wooded country and up to Canteleu. From the church terrace here there is a good if limited view of Rouen's port and some of the town.

Lunch at Rouen.

Forges-les-Eaux

Gradually the route turns back to the Normandy coast (N28/D919), first stopping at Forges-les-Eaux on the River Epte. The town, as its name suggests, was once an iron-working centre. Charcoal for the furnaces was extracted from the Bray forest. It is charmingly laid out but not particularly remarkable except that it is a road centre and one of the nearest spas and health resorts to Paris. The waters (supposed to cure anaemia) are only used for drinking. There is a buvette at the entrance to the spa park. Louis XIII, his queen and Cardinal Richelieu came here to take the waters, which were supposed to cure the queen's alleged sterility. Louis XIV was born six years later! Three of the mineral waters were named 'La Royale', 'La Reinette' and 'la Cardinale'. You can visit a museum called Musée de l'Age d'Or and a collection of pottery in the Hotel de Ville.

Continue north (D1314) to Neufchâtel-en-Bray — the centre of cream cheese production but remarkable for little else. The Mathon-Durand Museum of arts and heritage is housed in a 16th-century building. Here one is shown the stages of production of the famous Bondon cheese. Outside is a cider mill and press.

Further north the Yères valley (D1314/D16) provides a pleasant wooded drive. The valley ends at Criel-Plage, then Mesnil-Val, about 15 miles north of Dieppe, both have pleasing pebble coves, set picturesquely in wooded surroundings between cliffs. Good bathing is to be had at each and there is sand at low tide.

Le Tréport

Le Tréport about 5 miles away on Normandy's northern border can be rather crowded in season, especially with Parisians. It has all the amenities of a larger resort — shops, restaurants, swimming pool and colourful Sunday open-air market — also 16th-century church, pebble beach and small fishing port at the mouth of the Bresle river. Its position guaranteed it a history of attack and destruction, especially by the English in the Hundred Years' War, but happily, more latterly, it early became a favourite sea-bathing resort. Louis-Philippe,

France's citizen king who patronised it regularly during his short 19th-century reign, helped to popularise it.

Dinner and overnight at Le Tréport.

Hôtel de Picardie
Place de la Gare
76470 Le Tréport
Tel: 35 86 02 22

This hotel overlooks the harbour and the steep cliffs towering behind. Reasonably priced and interesting menu.

Closed:	Open all year except Sunday evenings and Mondays
Rooms:	30
Facilities:	Restaurant
Credit cards:	Carte Bleue, Eurocard, Mastercard
Food:	Medaillon de lotte au coulis d'écrevisses
Rating:	★★★

USEFUL INFORMATION: NEUFCHÂTEL-EN-BRAY

Tourist Office:	6 Place Notre Dame
	(July-August)
	Tel: 35 93 22 96
	or The Town Hall
	Tel: 35 93 00 85
Population:	5,823

USEFUL INFORMATION: LE TRÉPORT

Tourist Office:	Esplanade Plage
	Tel: 35 86 05 69
Population:	6,555
Amenities:	Casinos, old port, swimming pool and wind surfing

Recipes from the Region

MENU 1 &

Soup à l'Oseille
Sorrel Soup

. . .

Lapin à la Cauchoise
Rabbit with Cream and Mustard Sauce

. . .

Soufflé à la Normande
Norman Apple Soufflé

* *Wine suggestion*
A light red wine from the Loire, e.g. Bourgeuil
or Saumur-Champigny

---

* In the menus that follow we suggest wines to
accompany the meals, however this is only done in
deference to common practice. Strictly speaking one
should always drink cider or Calvados with a Norman
meal.

Soupe à l'Oseille
Sorrel Soup

2oz/50g butter
1 medium onion,
chopped
2 large handfuls sorrel,
stalks removed and
chopped
1 large potato, cubed
1½ pint/900ml chicken
stock
salt and pepper
cream (optional)

Serves 4

Melt the butter, cook the onion until pale yellow, then add the sorrel and stir until it turns dark. Add the potato and stock, season with salt and pepper, cover and simmer for 30 minutes. Purée the soup in a liquidizer or processor or put it through a food mill. Taste for seasoning. If you wish, stir a spoonful of cream into each serving.

Lapin à la Cauchoise
Rabbit with Cream and Mustard Sauce

1 rabbit, cut into
serving pieces
2oz/50g butter
6 tbs crème fraîche*
salt and pepper
3 tbs Dijon mustard
2 shallots, chopped
finely
¼ pint/150ml dry cider

Serves 4

Brown the rabbit pieces on all sides in the butter, then take them from the pan and discard the butter. Put 2 tbs of the crème fraîche into the pan, put back the rabbit and turn the pieces so they are well coated with the cream. Season with salt and pepper. Cover the pan and cook very gently for 40 minutes, adding another tablespoon of cream every 10 minutes.

* A note on crème fraîche
I have used crème fraîche in the recipes because it is now possible to buy it in some supermarkets and delicatessens. If you can't get it, use double or whipping cream and add a teaspoon or so of lemon juice to give the cream the slightly sour taste which is a characteristic of crème fraîche.

While the rabbit is cooking mix together the mustard, shallots and cider. Pour this mixture over the rabbit with the last spoonful of cream and cook for another 15–20 minutes, then serve.

Soufflé à la Normande
Norman Apple Soufflé

2 russet apples
5 tbs Calvados
4 fl oz/100ml milk
1 tbs flour
3 tbs castor sugar
½oz/10g butter
2 egg yolks
3 egg whites
icing sugar

Serves 4

Peel, core and dice the apples and macerate in 3 tbs Calvados for 2 hours. Butter a 1¾ pint/1 litre soufflé dish and dust it with sugar. Pour a tablespoon of the milk on to the flour and blend together, then pour the rest of the milk into a pan, add the sugar and bring to the boil. Stir in the flour and milk, and cook for a few minutes until the mixture thickens slightly. Take the pan from the heat and stir in the butter, egg yolks and remaining Calvados. Whisk the egg whites to firm peaks and gently fold them into the mixture.

Spoon a thin layer of the soufflé mixture into the dish and sprinkle 2–3 tbs of the diced apple over it. Make more layers of soufflé mixture and apple, finishing with a layer of soufflé mixture. Cook in a preheated oven — 180°C/250°F/gas 4 for 30 minutes. At the end of cooking time sprinkle a little icing sugar over the top of the soufflé, turn the oven to its highest temperature and put back the soufflé for 2–3 minutes until the top is nicely glazed.

MENU 2 &

Terrine de Canard à la Rouennaise
Duck Terrine

. . .

Marmite Dieppoise
Dieppe Fish Stew

. . .

Fraises et Framboises marinées au Calvados
Strawberries and Raspberries in Calvados

. . .

Wine suggestion
A modest red Burgundy e.g. Mercurey or
Montagny *or* a Sancerre or Pouilly if you prefer
white wine with the fish course.

Terrine de Canard à la Rouennaise
Duck Terrine, as prepared in Rouen

1 duck weighing about
4lb/2kg
8oz/250g lean pork,
diced
12oz/375g pork back
fat, diced
the duck liver, cleaned
½oz/10g butter
1 small onion, chopped
finely
2 tsp salt
black pepper
ground ginger
dried thyme
nutmeg
1 tbs Calvados
1 egg
strips of back fat or
streaky bacon rashers

Serves 10

Strip all the duck meat from the carcass. Grind the meat, fat and skin with the pork and pork fat and the liver in a food processor. Work in small batches.

Melt the butter in a small pan and soften the onion. Let it cool then add it to the meat with the salt, lots of freshly ground black pepper, a couple of good pinches each of ground ginger and dried thyme and a grating of nutmeg. Put in the Calvados and the egg and mix thoroughly with your hands.

Line the bottom and sides of a terrine with most of the back fat or streaky bacon. Put in the meat mixture, mounding it up in the middle and cover the top with the remaining strips of fat. Cover the terrine with a lid or with foil.

Preheat the oven to 160°C/325°F/gas 3. Place the terrine in a baking tin and pour round it about an inch of hot water. Cook for 2½ hours, checking occasionally that the water does not need replenishing.

Remove the terrine from the oven and let it cool slowly before putting it in the refrigerator. Serve cold with small gherkins and some good bread.

Marmite Dieppoise
Dieppe Fish Stew

5lb/2.5kg firm white
fish — sole, flounder,
gurnard, halibut, turbot,
haddock etc, cleaned
and cut into largish
pieces
2 leeks, white part only,
chopped
3 shallots, chopped
1 medium onion,
chopped
6oz/150g mushrooms,
chopped
2oz/50g butter
3 tbs flour
bouquet garni
2lb/1kg mussels,
scrubbed and cleaned
½ pint/300ml crème
fraîche
salt and pepper
chopped parsley to
garnish

for the fish stock
heads, bones and
trimmings from fish
2 stalks celery, chopped
1 medium onion,
chopped
2 leeks, green part,
chopped
1 bay leaf
1 sprig thyme
a few parsley stalks
8 black peppercorns,
crushed
¼ pint/150ml dry white
wine or cider
salt

Chop the fish bones into 2 or 3 pieces and put all the ingredients for the stock into a large pan. Cover and cook gently for 5 minutes. Pour in 3½ pints/2 litres water, bring to the boil, then lower the heat and simmer, skimming as necessary, for 30 minutes. Strain and refrigerate if you aren't going to use the stock straight away.

Melt the butter in a large pan and cook the vegetables slowly for 10–15 minutes until they have softened but not browned. Sprinkle on the flour and stir in. Pour in 1¾ pints/1 litre of the fish stock. Stir well and bring to the boil. Add the bouquet garni, season with salt and pepper and simmer for 10 minutes. Put the pieces of fish into the stew and simmer for 5 minutes, then add the mussels and continue to simmer for a further 10 minutes. Lift out the fish and mussels with a slotted spoon and put them into a warm tureen. Discard any mussels that haven't opened. Pour the cream into the liquid, stir it through, check the seasoning and add the chopped parsley. Pour over the dish and serve.

Serves 8

Fraises et Framboises marinées au Calvados

Strawberries and Raspberries in Calvados

1lb/500g small
strawberries
1lb/500g raspberries
6 tbs castor sugar
6 tbs Calvados
½ pint/300ml double
cream

Serves 8

Put the fruit into a serving bowl, preferably glass, sprinkle 2 tbs sugar over it and add the Calvados. Leave to steep in the refrigerator for at least 1 hour. Whip the cream with the remaining sugar until it is stiff, then fold it into the fruit. Keep cold until you are ready to serve.

MENU 3 &

Moules à la Crème
Mussels in Cream Sauce

. . .

Gigot d'Agneau Pré-salé
Leg of Salt Meadow Lamb

. . .

Tarte au Fromage Blanc
Cheese Tart

. . .

Wine suggestion
A red Bordeaux from one of the small châteaux.

Moules à la Crème
Mussels in Cream Sauce

4lb/2kg mussels
4 tbs dry white wine or cider
2 tbs chopped onion
2 egg yolks
pinch of pepper
¼pt/150ml double cream
¼ tsp lemon juice
2 tbs chopped parsley
salt

Serves 6–8

Wash the mussels in cold water, scrub well and remove beards. In a large pot bring ¼pt/150ml water, the white wine, and the onion to the boil. Add the mussels, cover, and steam for approximately 5 minutes. Remove the mussels with a slotted spoon, and discard any that have not opened. Remove the shells and keep the mussels warm.

Reduce the cooking liquid over high heat for 3 to 4 minutes. Strain through a fine sieve into a smaller pan.

Whisk together the egg yolks, pepper, cream, lemon juice, and chopped parsley. Pour the mixture into the reduced cooking liquor over low heat, stirring constantly for a few minutes until it thickens. Do not let the sauce boil. Taste to see if any salt is necessary.

Transfer the mussels to a serving bowl, pour the hot sauce over them and serve with lots of good French bread.

Gigot d'Agneau Pré-salé
Leg of Salt Meadow Lamb

6lb/3kg leg of lamb
salt and pepper
2oz/50g butter
1 large onion, chopped
1 large carrot, chopped
½ pint/300ml stock

Serves 6–8

Season the lamb with salt and pepper, rub the surface with butter and put it in a roasting tin. Preheat the oven to 230°C/450°F/gas 8. Roast the meat for 20 minutes, turning and basting it frequently. Lower the heat to 190°C/380°F/gas 5, arrange the vegetables around the lamb and pour a little of the stock over it. Roast for an hour more if you like your lamb pink, 1 hour 15 minutes if you like it well done, basting often with the juices.

Remove the lamb from the oven and let it rest in a warm place for 20 minutes to concentrate the juices in the flesh. Meanwhile skim some of the fat from the roasting tin, put the tin over medium heat and add the rest of the stock. Boil for a few minutes, mashing the vegetables into the stock, until the stock has reduced a little. Season to taste, then strain the gravy into a sauceboat and serve separately.

Tarte au Fromage Blanc
Cheese Tart

for the pastry
4oz/120g butter
8oz/250g plain flour
2 tbs sugar
1 egg
salt
2–3 tbs cold water

12oz/350g curd cheese
6 tbs crème fraîche
4 tbs castor sugar
1 tsp grated lemon zest
3 eggs

Serves 6-8

Cut the butter into small pieces. Sift flour, sugar and a pinch of salt into a mixing bowl. Make a well in the centre, and add the butter and egg. Work together to make a soft paste, incorporating some of the cold water if necessary. Roll into a ball and chill for 30 minutes.

Roll out the pastry and line a 10in/25cm tart tin with a removable base. Prick the bottom of the tart with a fork in several places, line with foil and parbake in a preheated 180°C/350°F/gas 4 oven for 5 minutes. Take the tart shell from the oven and remove the foil.

While the shell is baking, prepare the cheese filling. Mix the curd cheese with the crème fraîche and beat well until it is smooth. Stir in the sugar and lemon zest and add the eggs, one at a time, beating well.

Pour the cheese mixture into the tart shell, lower the oven temperature to 160°C/320°F/gas 3 and bake for 40 minutes or until a skewer inserted in the middle comes out clean. Serve hot, warm or cold.

MENU 4 &

Crevettes au Cidre
Shrimps in Cider

. . .

Filets de Sole à la Normande
Normandy Sole

. . .

Sorbet aux Pommes
Apple Sorbet with Calvados

. . .

Wine suggestion
Muscadet — look for Muscadet-sur-lie (bottled
straight from the lees) for greater flavour.

Crevettes au Cidre
Shrimps in Cider

1lb/500g small raw
shrimps
¾ pint/450ml dry cider
salt and pepper
bouquet garni

Serves 4

Put the cider and an equal quantity of water to
boil with the salt, pepper and bouquet garni. Let
it boil for 10 minutes then tip in the shrimps.
Bring back to the boil and cook for 5 minutes.
Drain and serve hot with bread and butter.

Filets de Sole à la Normande
Normandy Sole

3lb/1.5kg Dover sole,
filleted
salt and pepper
4fl oz/100ml dry cider
¼ pint/150ml crème
fraîche

Serves 4

This is the simplest version of the classic
Norman dish. You may add sautéd mushrooms,
opened mussels or oysters at the same time as
the cream if you want a grander version.

Butter a gratin or similar dish that will take the
fillets in a single layer. Put in the fish, season
with salt and pepper and pour over the cider.
Cover and cook in a preheated oven — 180°C/
350°F/gas 4 for 10 minutes. Now pour over the
crème fraîche, baste the fish and cook for a
further 10 minutes. Serve at once.

Sorbet aux Pommes
Apple Sorbet with Calvados

8oz/250g sugar
¾ pint/450ml water
5 green eating apples,
such as Granny Smiths

Bring the sugar and water to the boil. Peel, core
and quarter the apples and add them to the
syrup with the lemon zest and juice. Simmer
very gently for 30–40 minutes until the apples

143

zest of 1 lemon
1 tbs lemon juice
6 tbs Calvados

Serves 4

are soft. Take the pan from the heat and leave the apples to cool in the syrup. When cold, purée in the food processor or liquidizer.

Turn into an ice cream maker and freeze according to the manufacturer's instructions. If you don't have an ice cream machine, put the mixture in the freezer and as soon as it begins to freeze, beat it well for 1 minute. Put it back in the freezer and repeat twice more at 30 minute intervals.

Keep the sorbet frozen until ready to serve, then scoop it into balls, arrange in individual glasses and sprinkle with Calvados.

MENU 5 ❦

Rillettes

. . .

Poulet Vallée d'Auge
Chicken with Cream

. . .

Tarte aux Pommes Normande
Normandy Apple Tart

. . .

Wine suggestion
A Beaujolais or a red country wine such as
Bergerac or Côtes de Buzet from the south-west.

Rillettes

1lb/500g belly pork
½lb/250g pork back fat
bouquet garni
salt and pepper
quatre-épices or other
spices to taste

Serves 6

To make good rillettes, the pork must be cooked very slowly so that it is very soft and 'melting'.

Cut the meat and fat into thin strips, like matchsticks and put them in a heavy pan with a ladleful of water. Add the bouquet garni, put the pan over a very low heat, cover and simmer for 3½–4 hours. Check from time to time to see that the meat is not sticking; add a little more water if necessary.

When the meat is very soft, discard the bouquet garni and remove the meat from the fat and liquid. Put the meat in a food processor, or drop onto the blades of a liquidizer, to shred it. Take care not to work the machine for too long, or you will end up with purée.

Meanwhile, reduce the liquid in the pan for 20 or 30 minutes. Essentially, you are boiling off the water and clarifying the fat, and the fat should look transparent.

Cool the fat a little, then add it, a little at a time, to the shredded meat, tasting as you go. Season with salt, pepper and quatre-épices, or other spices of your choice. The texture of rillettes should be smooth and soft. Refrigerate until needed, but remove from the refrigerator in advance of serving because rillettes should not be too cold.

Poulet Vallée d'Auge
Chicken from the Auge Valley

4lb/2kg chicken
4oz/120g unsalted
butter
salt, pepper
4–5 tbs Calvados
½pt/300ml crème
fraîche

Serves 6

Cut the chicken into pieces. Heat the butter in a sauté pan or casserole, put in the chicken and brown on all sides. Season with salt and pepper. Reduce the heat, cover the pan and cook very slowly for about an hour, or until the chicken is tender.

Warm the Calvados in a ladle or small pan, set it alight and pour it over the chicken. Stir well. When the flames have died out, remove the chicken pieces to a warm platter and keep hot.

Pour the crème fraîche into the pan, stir briskly and bring to the boil. Lower the heat and simmer for about 5 minutes until the sauce has thickened. Pour it over the chicken and serve.

Tarte aux Pommes Normande
Normandy Apple Tart

12oz/350g puff pastry
1lb/500g good eating
apples, peeled, cored
and sliced thinly
4oz/120g flour
4oz/120g almonds,
blanched and chopped
6oz/175g castor sugar
ground cinnamon
4oz/120g butter

Serves 6

Roll out the puff pastry to line a 10in/25cm tart tin, preferably one with a removable base. Fill the pastry case with the apples. In a bowl mix together the flour, almonds, sugar and a good pinch of cinnamon, then rub in the butter with your fingertips until the mixture looks like fine crumbs. Cover the apples with the crumb mixture and bake in a preheated oven at 200°C/400°F/gas 6 for 35–40 minutes.

Glossary of Food Terms

Starters

charcuterie	cold meats (pork)
crudités	raw vegetables
escargots	snails
potage	soup
terrine	a type of coarse pâté

Meats (Viande)

agneau (gigot de)	lamb (leg of)
boeuf (filet de)	beef (fillet steak)
bleu	very rare
saignant	rare
à point	medium
bien cuit	well done
brochette	kebab
côte/côtelette	chop
entrecôte	steak (rib)
jambon	ham
lapin	rabbit
lièvre	hare
mouton	mutton
saucisse	sausage (fresh)
saucisson	sausage (dry)
veau	veal

Offal (Abats)

boudin	black pudding
cervelle	brains
foie	liver
langue	tongue
ris	sweetbreads
rognon	kidney

Poultry (Volaille) and Game (Gibier)

caille	quail
canard/caneton	duck/duckling

coq	cockerel
faisan	pheasant
oie	goose
perdrix	partridge
pintade	guinea fowl
poulet	chicken
sanglier	wild boar

Fish (Poisson) and Shellfish (Crustacés/Coquillages)

alose	shad
anguilles (en gelée)	eels (jellied)
bouquet	prawn
brochet	pike
cabillaud	cod
coquilles St. Jacques	scallops
crevettes	prawns/shrimps
écrevisse	crayfish
fruits de mer	mixed shellfish
hareng	herring
homard	lobster
huitres	oyster
langoustine	scampi
lamproie	lamphrey
lotte	monkfish
loup de mer	sea bass
maquereau	mackerel
moules	mussels
saumon	salmon
truite	trout

Vegetables (Légumes)

ail	garlic
artichaut	artichoke (globe)
asperge	asparagus
carotte	carrot
champignon	mushroom
chou	cabbage
choucroute	sauerkraut
choufleur	cauliflower
épinards	spinach
haricots verts	French beans
navet	turnip
oignon	onion

149

Travels in Normandy

pomme de terre	potato
au four	baked, roast
purée	mashed
petits pois	peas
poireau	leek
poivron	green/red pepper
riz	rice

Fruit

ananas	pineapples
cassis	blackcurrant
cerise	cherry
citron	lemon
fraise	strawberry
framboise	raspberry
groseille	redcurrant
mûr	blackberry
pamplemousse	grapefruit
pêche	peach
poire	pear
pomme	apple
prune	plum

Selected Bibliography

WILLIAM THE FIRST AND THE NORMAN CONQUEST by Frank Barlow, E.U.P.

THE NORMAN ACHIEVEMENT by David C. Douglas, Eyre & Spottiswoode.

WILLIAM THE CONQUEROR by David C. Douglas, Eyre & Spottiswoode, 1964.

CRUSADE IN EUROPE by Dwight D. Eisenhower, Heinemann, 1948.

MADAME BOVARY by Gustave Flaubert, Translated by Gerard Hopkins, Oxford University Press, World Classics, 1959.

THE IMPRESSIONISTS by William Gaunt, Thames & Hudson, 1970.

THE SEINE by Anthony Glyn, Weidenfeld and Nicholson, 1966.

NORMANDY by Peter Gunn, Gollancz, 1975.

NORMANS IN EUROPEAN HISTORY by Charles Homer Haskins, Constable, 1914.

MADELINE, YOUNG WIFE by Mrs Robert Henrey, Dent, 1960.

GUY DE MAUPASSANT, native of region, set many of his short stories in Normandy.

NORMANDY, Michelin, English edition, The Dickens Press.

NORMANDY TO THE BALTIC by Viscount Montgomery, Hutchinsons, 1946.

OUR GUEST PAID IN FRANCE by Len Ortzen, Phoenix House, 1953.

60 MILES FROM ENGLAND (THE ENGLISH AT DIEPPE, 1814–1914) by Simon Pakenham, Macmillan, 1967.

AN OUTLINE OF EUROPEAN ARCHITECTURE by Nikolaus Pevsner, John Murray.

PORTRAIT OF NORMANDY by Derek Pitt and Michael Shaw, Hale, 1974.

THE BASTARD KING by Jean Plaidy, Hale, 1974.

COMPANION GUIDE TO NORMANDY by Nesta Roberts, Collins, 1980.

THE BAYEUX TAPESTRY by Sir Frank Stenton, Phaidon Press, 1957.

NORMANDY by Barbara Whelpton, Spur Books, 1975.

Geographical Index

Index of Recipes

Other Merehurst Travel Titles

TRAVELS IN THE DORDOGNE
TRAVELS IN PROVENCE
TRAVELS IN TUSCANY
TRAVELS IN NORMANDY

All the titles in the series offer the reader a ten/twelve day journey
through the region pointing out places of interest, hotels and restaurants
with special emphasis on the food and wines of the area.
Each book also contains a mapped itinerary with distances and times for
each day of the journey.
As well as hints and tips on what to buy and eat in the region readers
are provided with a selection of recipes and menus which they can use on
their return to form a lasting memory of their visit.

All titles now available from bookshops or direct from Merehurst
Publishing, 5 Great James Street, London WC1N 3DA at £6.95, plus
£1.00 post and packing.

SETTING UP IN FRANCE

For everyone who is interested in buying, leasing, renting or time-sharing in France.

This book will cover everything from raising the money to installing water, gas, electricity, planning permissions and much more in urban and rural sites throughout France.

Written by Laetitia de Warren, the French born editor of Le Magazine, this will become 'the' reference book on the subject.

Now available from booksellers at £9.95 or direct from the publisher at £9.95 plus £1.00 post and packing.